中华五福吉祥图典
Designs of Chinese Blessings

禄

High Salary

黄全信　黄　迎 / 主　编
周　晔 / 翻　译

华语教学出版社
SINOLINGUA

First Edition 2003

Revised Edition 2015

First Printing 2015

ISBN 978-7-5138-0924-5
Copyright 2015 by Sinolingua Co., Ltd
Published by Sinolingua Co., Ltd
24 Baiwanzhuang Road, Beijing 100037, China
Tel: (86) 10-68320585 68997826
Fax: (86) 10-68997826 68326333
http://www.sinolingua.com.cn
E-mail: hyjx@sinolingua.com.cn
Facebook: www.facebook.com/sinolingua
Printed by Beijing Tianyuxing Printing House

Printed in the People's Republic of China

目 录
Contents

1 / 人臻五福　花满三春
　　May People Enjoy a Life Full of Blessings
　　and May Flowers Bloom Throughout the Spring

8 / 一甲一名
　　Number One scholar

14 / 一品当朝
　　Highest ranking official

16 / 一品清廉
　　Virtuous high-ranking official

18 / 一琴一鹤
　　One *qin* and one crane

20 / 一路连科
　　Continual success in examinations

22 / 一路荣华
　　Glory all one's life

26 / 二甲传胪
　　The enumeration of top students

28 / 八　骏　马
　　Eight fine horses

30 / 九　　　章
　　Nine decorative patterns

32 / 九　　锡
The emperor's nine gifts

34 / 九　　雏
Nine nestlings

36 / 三　　清
Three Taoist Gods

38 / 三元五福
Three top students and five happinesses

42 / 三元及第
Three top students in the imperial examinations

44 / 三元报喜
The announcement of a top student in the imperial examinations

46 / 大人虎变
Unpredictable changes of powerful people

48 / 孔子讲学
Confucius teaching

50 / 夕牛望日
An old ox looks at the sun

52 / 马上封侯
Immediately become a high official

54 / 云龙风虎
Dragon of the cloud, tiger of the wind

56 / 太师少师
Old and young imperial teachers

58 / 太师童子
Old and young imperial teachers

60 / 五　　瑞
Five propitious kinds of jade

62 / 五子登科
Five sons passing the imperial examinations

64 / 五子连登
   Five sons passing the imperial examinations
66 / 五子连科
   Five sons passing the imperial examinations
68 / 五子日升
   Five sons like the rising sun
70 / 五子夺冠
   Five sons become champions
72 / 五子夺莲
   Five sons compete for the lotus
74 / 五子夺魁
   Five sons become top students
76 / 丹凤朝阳
   The phoenix flies towards the sun
78 / 凤鸣朝阳
   The phoenix sings towards the sun
80 / 朝阳鸣凤
   The sun rises and the phoenixes sing
82 / 文武状元
   Number One scholars
84 / 文官补子
   The decoration of a civil official's uniform
86 / 武官补子
   The decoration of a military official's uniform
88 / 夫荣妻贵
   A glorious husband, a noble wife
90 / 玉树芝兰
   The noble magnolia, irises and orchids
92 / 玉树临风
   Magnolia faces the wind

目录

Contents

94 / 平升三级
Be promoted three grades in succession
98 / 四艺集雅
Four civilized arts
100 / 加官进禄
Promotion and salary increase
106 / 加官进爵
Promotion
110 / 玄女送子
A child-sending goddess
112 / 百忍图
The picture of great tolerance
114 / 百禄图
A picture of great wealth and good fortune
116 / 百鸟朝凤
One hundred birds pay tribute to the phoenix
118 / 芝兰竟秀
Irises and orchids compete
120 / 当朝一品
The Number One government official
122 / 如意状元
Number One candidate
124 / 伦叙图
A picture of ethical standards
126 / 旭日东升
The sun rises from the east
128 / 兰桂齐芳
The orchid and the sweet-scented osmanthus blossom together

130 / 负薪读书
　　Study from the shoulder pole
132 / 红杏尚书
　　Red apricot minister
136 / 鸡群鹤立
　　A crane among roosters
138 / 苍龙江牙
　　The green dragon among the tide
140 / 连中三元
　　Continuous success
144 / 连升三级
　　Continuous promotion
146 / 状元及第
　　The Number One scholar is announced
150 / 状元游街
　　The Number One scholar parading in the street
152 / 状元祝寿
　　The Number One scholar celebrating his birthday
154 / 君子豹变
　　Great changes in position
156 / 平步青云
　　Stepping over blue clouds
158 / 青龙盘柱
　　The green dragon surrounding the pillar
160 / 青钱万选
　　Selecting bronze coins from among the pile
162 / 青狮荣华
　　The lion brings high position and great wealth
164 / 英雄斗志
　　The ambition of the hero

目录

Contents

166 / 英雄独立
　　The independent spirit of the hero
168 / 虎威子孙
　　Tigers to guard the children
170 / 鱼龙变化
　　A fish turning into a dragon
172 / 官上加官
　　Continuous promotion
178 / 官居一品
　　The highest ranking official
180 / 春风得意
　　Riding over the crest to success
182 / 春花三杰
　　Three spring flowers
184 / 封侯挂印
　　Winning the title of duke and the official stamp
186 / 带子上朝
　　Bringing the son to the palace
190 / 指日高升
　　Major promotion in a short period
194 / 独占鳌头
　　The top student in the examination
198 / 香花三元
　　The three fragrant flowers
200 / 洞天一品
　　The greatest Dong Tian stone
202 / 前程万里
　　Great expectations
204 / 冠带流传
　　Retain official titles through the generations

208 / 鸾鸟绶带
Golden bird presenting a ribbon

210 / 高官厚禄
High position and good salary

212 / 捧圭朝天
Holding jade and facing the sky

214 / 翎顶辉煌
The brilliance of peacock plumes and coral

216 / 红顶花翎
A red hat with peacock plumes

218 / 海水江牙
Towering peak among the roaring waves

220 / 喜报三元
Magpie announcing the passing of three examinations

222 / 喜得连科
Happily pass the palace examination

224 / 辈辈封侯
Official position held through generations

226 / 魁星点斗
Kwei Star pointing to the Big Dipper

228 / 禄星高照
The star symbolizing salary shines above

230 / 猿猴托印
The monkey brings official position

232 / 富寿年丰
Enjoy wealth, longevity and good harvests

234 / 鲤跃龙门
The carp jumping over the dragon gate

236 / 禄位高升
Promotion to an official position

目录
Contents

238 / 攀桂乘龙
    Passing the palace examination and getting happily married
240 / 蟾宫折桂
    Pluck osmanthus blossoms from the moon
242 / 麒麟送子
    Kylin bringing sons

High Salary
Designs of Chinese Blessings

人臻五福　　花满三春

　　吉祥一词，始见于《易经》："吉事有祥。"《左传》有："是何祥也？吉祥焉在？"《庄子》则有："虚室生日，吉祥止止。"《注疏》亦云："吉者，福善之事；祥者，嘉庆之征。"

　　吉祥二字，在甲骨文中被写作"吉羊"。上古人过着游牧生活，羊肥大成群是很"吉祥"的事，在古器物的铭文中多有"吉羊"。《说文》云："羊，祥也。"

　　吉祥，是美好、幸运的形象；吉祥，是人类最迷人的主题。艺术最终都是把理想形象化，而吉祥图，是中华吉祥文化最璀璨的明珠。旧时有联："善果皆欢喜，香云普吉祥。"吉祥图有：吉祥如意、五福吉祥等。

　　五福，是吉祥的具体体现。福、禄、寿、喜、财，在民间被称为五福；福星、禄星、寿星、喜神、财神，在仙界被尊为五福神。五福最早见于《尚书》："五福，一曰寿，二曰富，三曰康宁，四曰攸好德，五曰考终命。"旧时有联："三阳临吉地，五福萃华门。"吉祥图有：五福捧寿、三多五福等。

　　福，意为幸福美满。《老子》："福兮，祸所伏。"《韩

非子》:"全富贵之谓福。"旧时有联:"香焚一炷,福赐三多。"吉祥图有:福在眼前、纳福迎祥、翘盼福音、天官赐福等。

禄,意为高官厚禄。《左传》:"介之推不言禄,禄亦弗及。"《汉书》:"身宠而载高位,家温而食厚禄。"旧时有联:"同科十进士,庆榜三名元。"吉祥图有:禄位高升、福禄寿喜、天赐禄爵、加官进禄等。

寿,意为健康长寿。《庄子》:"人,上寿百岁,中寿八十,下寿六十。"《诗经》:"如南山之寿,不骞不崩。"旧时有联:"同臻寿域,共跻春台。"吉祥图有:寿星高照、鹤寿千年、富贵寿考、蟠桃献寿等。

喜,意为欢乐喜庆。《国语》:"固庆其喜而吊其忧。"韦昭注:"喜犹福也。"旧时有联:"笑到几时方合口,坐来无日不开怀。"吉祥图有:喜上眉梢、双喜临门、端阳喜庆、皆大欢喜等。

财,意为发财富有。《荀子》:"务本节用财无极。"旧时有联:"生意兴隆通四海,财源茂盛达三江。"吉祥图有:财源滚滚、招财进宝、喜交财运、升官发财等。

吉祥图不仅有"五福"之内涵,而且与绘画艺术和语言艺术珠联璧合。在绘画上,吉祥图体现了中国画主要的表现手段——线的魅力,给人以美感,令人赏心悦目。吉祥图虽多出自民间画工之手,却多有顾恺之"春蚕吐丝"之韵,曹仲达"曹衣出水"之美,吴道子"吴带当风"之妙。在语言上,吉祥图使古代文化通俗化和普及化,吉祥图多配有一句浓缩成四个字的吉语祥词,给人以吉祥的祝愿,令人心驰神往。

《中华五福吉祥图典》,汇集了我的数代家传和几十年收藏的精品吉祥图,可谓美不胜收。其中既有明之典雅,又有清之华丽;既有皇家之富贵,又有民间之淳朴;既有北方之粗犷,又有南方之秀美……全套书按五福分成福、

High Salary
Designs of Chinese Blessings

禄、寿、喜、财五集，每集吉祥图119幅，共595幅。除同类图案外，全套书均按笔画顺序编排，基本包括了中国传统吉祥图的各个方面，并对每幅图做了考证和诠释，力求图文并茂，相得益彰。

五福人人喜，吉祥家家乐。吉祥图是中国的，也是世界的，故以汉英对照出版。《中华五福吉祥图典》会给您带来吉祥，给您全家带来幸福。

黄全信于佩实斋

主编简介：

黄全信，满族，1944年出生于北京一个文化、书画世家，其父曾师承康有为。著名文化学者，中华传统文化研究会名誉会长；著名画家，中国书画家协会理事，中国书法家协会会员。多年来致力于中国传统文化艺术的研究，出版有关著作100余部。长期从事书画创作和美术教学工作，其书画作品多次参加国内外大展并获多个奖项；多次到日本、新加坡等地举办个人书画展；其书画作品被"台北故宫"和台湾"国父纪念馆"收藏。

黄迎，中国电影家协会会员、中国电影表演艺术学会会员。中国戏曲学院副教授、影视教研室主任。北京市青年拔尖人才、北京市中青年骨干教师。主编了20余部艺术著作，发表了20余篇艺术专业论文。

福禄寿喜财
中华五福吉祥图典

May People Enjoy a Life Full of Blessings and May Flowers Bloom Throughout the Spring

The word jíxiáng (meaning lucky, propitious, or auspicious) is used in ancient Chinese books and writings as early as the Zhou Dynasty (1100 -221BC).

The word jíxiáng was written 吉羊 (jíyáng, auspicious sheep) on oracle bones. To the ancient nomadic Chinese, large herds of well-fed sheep were prized possessions; the word jíyáng also appeared in engravings on ancient utensils.

To have good luck is an eternal desire of all people. As art records man's ideals, good luck pictures are the most illuminating part of Chinese spiritual culture. An old Chinese couplet says that kindness leads to happiness and good luck. Typical good luck pictures representing such include images depicting good luck and desire fulfilled to the heart's content, good luck with five blessings, etc.

The five blessings, good fortune, high salary and a good career, longevity, happiness, and wealth, are the major manifestations of good luck, with five different gods presiding over each. The five blessings as first mentioned in Chinese literature are not quite the same as the five which are spoken of today, though they are quite similar. A couplet says a prosperous family is granted many blessings. Typical good luck pictures representing such include: long-term enjoyment of all five

High Salary
Designs of Chinese Blessings

blessings, more blessings, etc.

Good fortune means happiness and complete satisfaction. Ancient Chinese philosophers, including Lao Zi, all commented on the notion of good fortune. Lao Zi once said fortune and adversity alternated with each other. An old couplet speaks of burning incense to ask for more blessings. Good luck pictures in this theme include: good fortune for today, hope for blessings, blessings from heaven, etc.

High salary means handsome salaries at a prestigious post. In ancient times, Chinese people attached great significance to academic excellence, which led in turn to high positions in government. An old couplet says, "May you distinguish yourself in the royal examinations and rank at the top of the list." Good luck pictures in this theme include: big improvements in salary and post; salary and position bestowed from heaven, etc.

Longevity refers to good health and a long life. As Zhuang Zi said, and as the *Book of Songs* records, longevity is the universal wish of mankind. As wished in an old couplet, to grow old together with a loved one is a joyful experience. This book has the following good luck pictures concerning longevity: high above shines the star of longevity; live to be 1000 years old with white hair; offering a Saturn peach to wish for longevity, etc.

Happiness refers to happy events and celebrations. According to ancient Chinese literature, happy events should be celebrated, while those with worries should be consoled. An old Chinese couplet says, "Why not keep on laughing as all days are filled with happiness?" Good luck pictures in this theme included in this book are double happiness arrives; all's well that ends well, etc.

Wealth means getting rich and satisfying material desires. The ancient Chinese people believed that the secret to endless wealth is to be down-to-earth and prudent. Illustrating the concept of wealth is an old couplet: A prosperous business deals with people from all corners of the world, then wealth rolls in from afar. Typical good luck pictures of this type include: in comes wealth; get rich and win high positions, etc.

Good luck pictures not only incorporate the five blessings, but the art of painting and language as well. The beautiful lines of these pictures, done in the style of traditional Chinese painting, provides the viewers with artistic enjoyment pleasing to the eye and heart; though mostly the work of folk artists, they exhibit a level of craftsmanship worthy of the great and famous masters. The language adopted in these pictures serves to popularize ancient culture and the four-character good luck phrase accompanying almost every picture depicts an attractive scene.

Designs of Chinese Blessings is a compilation of selected good luck pictures passed down in my family for several generations as well as those which I have been collecting for dozens of years. Their beauty is beyond description. They combine the elegance of the Ming Dynasty and the magnificence of the Qing Dynasty, the nobility of the royal family and the modesty of the common people, the boldness of the north and the delicacy of the south. The series consists of five volumes: *Good Fortune*, *High Salary and a Good Career*, *Longevity*, *Happiness* and *Wealth*. With 119 pictures in each volume, the whole series contains 595 pictures and is a complete representation of the various aspects of traditional Chinese good luck pictures. Pictures are arranged based on the stroke number of the first character of good luck phrases accompanying the picture. As well, research has been done on each picture, and the resulting interpretations complement the visuals nicely.

As the five blessings are the aspiration of each individual, good luck delights all households. Though the good luck pictures originate in China, their messages should benefit people all over the world. May the *Designs of Chinese Blessings* bring good luck to your life and happiness to your family.

Huang Quanxin

High Salary
Designs of Chinese Blessings

Introduction to Compilers:

  Huang Quanxin, of the Man ethnic group, was born into a Beijing family of culture, calligraphy and painting in 1944. His father was a disciple of Kang Youwei, who is well-known for advocating reform during the late Qing Dynasty. Huang is a famous scholar who specializes in culture studies and is the honorary president of the China Traditional Culture Studies Association. As a renowned calligrapher and painter, he became the director of the China Calligrapher and Painter Association, a member of China Calligraphers Association. He has been devoted to the study of traditional Chinese culture and art for many years, producing over 100 artistic works. He has also dedicated himself to the creation of painting and calligraphy works as well as instructing painters. Some of his artistic works have been displayed at the great exhibition halls at home and abroad and have received many awards. He has hosted several calligraphy and painting exhibitions in Japan and Singapore. Some of his artistic works were collected in Taipei's Palace Museum and the Sun Yat-sen Memorial Hall.

  Huang Ying is a member of China's Association of Film Professionals and China's Association of Film Performing. She is an associate professor and director of the Teaching and Research Office of TV and Film Performing at the National Academy of Chinese Theatre Arts. She is honored as the Outstanding Youth of Beijing in addition to the Middle-aged and Young Backbone Teacher of Beijing. She has compiled over 20 artistic works and published over 20 essays on art.

福禄寿喜财
中华五福吉祥图典

禄

一甲一名

Number One scholar

High Salary
Designs of Chinese Blessings

明、清科举考试，分乡试、会试、殿试三级。殿试考取三等称三甲，一甲前三名为状元、榜眼、探花。一甲一名即状元。"鸭"与"甲"谐，且一只为"一甲一名"。蟹有壳甲且一只亦为"一甲一名"。旧时对出远门的人送鸭或蟹，以祝前程远大。

There were three levels of imperial examination in the Ming and Qing dynasties: the county level, provincial level and the palace examination. There were also three grades for those who passed the highest imperial examination, with the title of Zhuàng Yuán (Number One), Bǎng Yǎn (Number Two) and Tàn Huā (Number Three). The words for duck and the shell of a crab sound like the best in Chinese. In old times, people gave ducks and crabs to those who would travel afar, wishing them great success.

福 禄 寿 喜 财
中华五福吉祥图典

禄

一甲一名

Number One scholar

High Salary
Designs of Chinese Blessings

图中的"芦"与"胪"谐音。科举时，殿试之后，皇帝传旨召见新考中的进士，依次唱名传呼，叫"胪唱"，也叫"传胪"、"胪传"。"胪唱曾叨殿上传，末班遥望御炉烟。""一甲一名"表示科举中第，而且是一等第一名。

Reed, as seen in the picture, sounds like enumeration in Chinese. After the palace examination, the emperor would send orders to meet those who had passed the examination one by one. This was called the enumeration. This term refers to the top student in the palace examination.

福 禄 寿 喜 财
中华五福吉祥图典

禄

一甲一名

Number One scholar

High Salary
Designs of Chinese Blessings

《汉书》："永光元年，……诏丞相、御史举质朴、敦厚、逊让、有行者，光禄岁以此科第郎、从官。"早在汉代就有了选拔、考核官吏的制度。"学而优则仕"，"万般皆下品，惟有读书高"。"一甲一名"是读书人的最高追求。

The history of using examinations to select officials can be traced back to the Han Dynasty. The Chinese in ancient times believed that those who excelled in study should become officials. Chinese people also believed that nothing could be compared to one's studies. To be the top student in a palace examination was always the utmost goal of all students.

福 禄 寿 喜 财
中华五福吉祥图典

禄

一品当朝
Highest ranking official

High Salary
Designs of Chinese Blessings

《国语·周语》:"外官不过九品。"皇帝手下的文武百官共分九级,是为九品。一品为最高一级,居人臣之极。一品文官的服饰为鹤。《花镜》:"鹤,一名仙鸟,羽族之长也。"也称一品鹤,仙鹤朝阳即"一品当朝",寓意官居极品。

There were nine levels of civil and military officials in Chinese feudal dynasties; these levels were called the nine grades. The decoration on the uniform of a top level civil official was a crane. The saying "crane bathing in the sunrise" was usually used to refer to very high-ranking officials.

福 禄 寿 喜 财
中华五福吉祥图典

禄

一品清廉

Virtuous high-ranking official

High Salary
Designs of Chinese Blessings

《群芳谱》:"凡物先华而后实,独此华实齐生,百节疏通,万窍玲珑,亭亭物华,出于淤泥而不染,花中之君子也。""莲"谐"廉",莲圣洁为"清",一莲喻一品。官分九品,一品为最高。"一品清廉"寓虽官居极品,却清明廉正。

The word for lotus is a homophone with integrity and honesty in Chinese. One lotus means the top ranking position. This term means that a top ranking official still maintains his integrity and honesty.

一琴一鹤

One qin and one crane

High Salary
Designs of Chinese Blessings

《宋史·赵抃传》:"赵抃号铁面刺史,帅蜀以一琴一鹤自随。"言赵抃刚直清廉,奉旨入蜀为高官,仅以一琴一鹤为伴。后世颂为官清廉,高雅不俗者,多以"一琴一鹤"誉之。古代,修身洁行且有时誉者被称为"鹤鸣之士。"

It was said that Zhao Bian (a high ranking official) only had one *qin* (an ancient musical instrument) and one crane as a companion, even when he was an official in Sichuan Province. One *qin* and one crane was later used to proclaim those high-ranking officials with great virtue.

福禄寿喜财
中华五福吉祥图典

一路连科

Continual success in examinations

High Salary
Designs of Chinese Blessings

鹭鸶又名白鹭,在古诗和吉祥画中常出现,为文人所喜。鹭也为明、清七品文官的补子纹样。芦苇生长时连棵成片,取其"连科"。又"莲"与"连"谐,也示"连科"。旧时科举考试,称连续考中为"连科"。以"一路连科"颂祝仕途顺利,一帆风顺。

The white heron was often referenced in ancient poems and paintings. White herons were adored by intellectuals and also used as the decoration of the uniform of officials of the seventh grade. Because lotus sounds like continuous in Chinese, the continuously growing lotus implies that students might continuously succeed in their examinations. This term also praises smooth progress in one's career.

福禄寿喜财
中华五福吉祥图典

禄

一路荣华

Glory all one's life

High Salary
Designs of Chinese Blessings

图中的一只鹭鸶表示"一路",芙蓉花表示"荣华"。王安石《拒霜花》诗赞芙蓉花:"群芳落尽独自芳。"芙蓉花是荣华勃发的象征,与牡丹合为"荣华富贵"。"一路荣华"与"一路连科"意近,"一路荣华"自然是一生享荣华、受富贵。

In this picture, the white heron represents going all the way and the confederate rose means glory as they are homophones, respectively in Chinese. The confederate rose and peony combined together are a symbol of prestige and wealth. This also has a meaning of smooth progress in one's career and the enjoyment of lifelong prestige and wealth.

福禄寿喜财
中华五福吉祥图典

禄

一路荣华

Glory all one's life

High Salary
Designs of Chinese Blessings

苏东坡《和述古拒霜花》："千林扫作一番黄，只有芙蓉独自芳；唤作拒霜知未称，看来却是最宜霜。"五代后蜀主孟昶于宫苑城头，尽植芙蓉，花开如锦，故称成都锦城、蓉城。"蓉"谐"荣"，"花"与"华"通假，与一鹭合为"一路荣华"。

Meng Chang, the last king of Sichuan Province in the Five Dynasties period, planted cotton-rose hibiscus all over his palace. Therefore, Chengdu (the modern capital city of Sichuan Province) was named "the city of the confederate rose". When confederate roses and white herons are used together it means endless prestige and wealth.

福 禄 寿 喜 财
中华五福吉祥图典

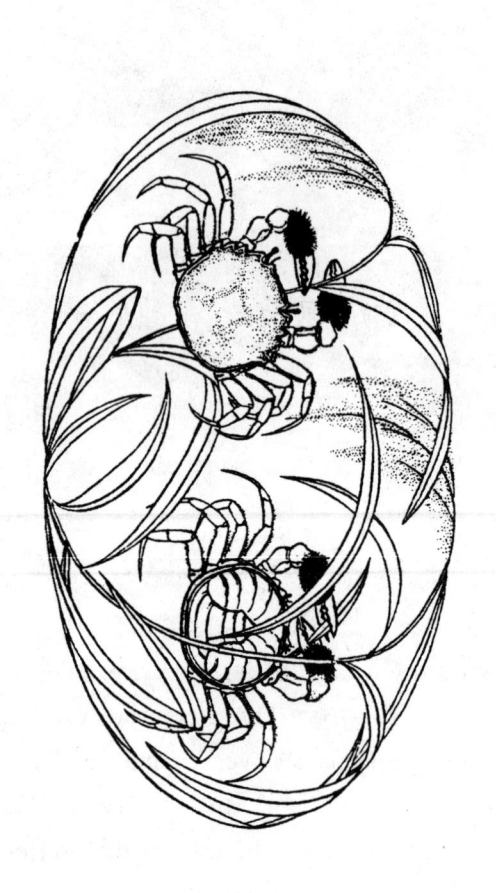

二甲传胪

The Enumeration of top students

High Salary
Designs of Chinese Blessings

旧时科举殿试，一甲第一名为状元，二甲第一名为传胪，三甲第一名亦称传胪。而金殿唱名也称之为传胪，传胪即科举中第。图中蟹有甲，故喻"二甲"，芦草之"芦"与"胪"谐音，故为"二甲传胪"，与一甲一名同意。

In the imperial examinations, the Number One student in top grade was called Zhuàng Yuán, while the Number One student in Grade Two and Grade Three were called Chuán Lú. The announcement of the successful candidates in the imperial palace was also called Chuán Lú. Here two crabs and reeds are used for their similar pronunciation to refer to those who passed the examination.

福禄寿喜财
中华五福吉祥图典

禄

八骏马
Eight fine horses

High Salary
Designs of Chinese Blessings

《穆天子传》:"天子之骏,赤骥、盗骊、白义、逾轮、山子、渠黄、华骝、绿耳。"郭璞注:"皆因其毛色以为名号耳。"八骏,是周穆王的八匹宝马良驹。古人常以骏马来比喻才华出众的人才,"八骏马"寓德才兼备、鸿图大展。

These eight horses were the eight precious horses of Duke Mu of the Zhou Dynasty. Ancient people often used fine horses as a metaphor for outstandingly talented people. The picture of eight horses refers to those who have outstanding capabilities and will fulfil their expectations.

福禄寿喜财
中华五福吉祥图典

禄

九 章
Nine decorative patterns

030

High Salary
Designs of Chinese Blessings

　　《周礼·春官·司服》载：古制王六服同冕；上公冕服九章，诸侯冕服七章，诸子冕服五章。《礼记·杂记上》云："复，诸侯以褒衣；冕服，爵弁服。"复，招魂之礼。九章类似十二章，是古代帝王冕服上的九种装饰图案。

　　It refers to the nine decorative patterns found on the ceremonial robes of ancient emperors.

福禄寿喜财
中华五福吉祥图典

禄

九　锡

The Emperor's nine gifts

High Salary
Designs of Chinese Blessings

《公羊传·庄公元年》:"加我服也",何休注:"礼有九锡:一曰车马,二曰衣服,三曰乐制,四曰朱户,五曰纳陛,六曰虎贲,七曰弓矢,八曰铁钺,九曰秬鬯。"九锡,是古代帝王赐给立大功或有权势的诸侯大臣的九种物品。

These are nine kinds of presents given to dukes or princes, and ministers who made significant contributions or were very powerful. They included a cart and horse, clothes, musical instruments, a bow and arrow, spear and battle axe, etc.

福禄寿喜财
中华五福吉祥图典

九　雏

Nine nestlings

High Salary
Designs of Chinese Blessings

　　《大戴礼·易本命》:"有羽之虫三百六十而凤凰为之长。"凤凰为百鸟之王,是祥瑞之鸟。《说文·隹部》:"雏,鸡子也。"段注:"引申为凡鸟子细小之称。"传说凤凰有九子,即九雏。后人多以九雏图赞誉美俊的有才少年。

　　The phoenix is considered to be the king of all birds by the Chinese. It was said that phoenix has nine sons, called Jiǔ Chú in Chinese. Later people used this term to refer to handsome and outstanding young men.

福禄寿喜财
中华五福吉祥图典

三 清
Three Taoist Gods

High Salary
Designs of Chinese Blessings

　　"三清"即道教玉清、上清、太清三清尊神。又指三尊居住三清天、三清境。在清皇室习俗中，农历正月初二，用梅花、松子、佛手加白雪烹制成"三清茶"，举行茶宴。传统文化中，以梅、松、佛手三件吉祥物，象征清明高洁。

　　The three gods of Taoism are Yu Qing, Shang Qing and Tai Qing, which also refer to the environments in which these three Taoist gods lived. In the Qing Dynasty royal family, people traditionally made Three Qing Tea on the second day of the first month according to the Chinese lunar calendar, which was made with plum blossom, pine seeds, fingered citron (Buddha's hand) and white snow, and held traditional tea parties. In Chinese traditional culture, plum blossom, pine and fingered citron are three symbols which stand for virtue and nobility.

三元五福

Three top students and five happinesses

High Salary
Designs of Chinese Blessings

旧时，贴于门上的吉祥画多成双、成对。"鸡"与"吉"谐音，表示大吉。童子手托元宝、花瓶，表示富贵平安。"三元及第"与"五福临门"合为"三元五福"。科举及第三元，是家长对子女的最大希望，是家中最为吉利的事情。

In old times, auspicious paintings came in pairs. Chickens stand for luck since they sound alike in Chinese. Children carrying a silver ingot and flower vase meant peace and wealth. The greatest wish of all parents for their children was that they should pass the palace examination; this was the luckiest thing that could befall a family.

三元五福

Three top students and five happinesses

High Salary
Designs of Chinese Blessings

梁朝《荆楚岁时记》:"正月一日,贴画鸡户上,悬苇索于其上,插桃符其傍,百鬼畏之。"门上贴鸡画镇宅由来已久,后来鸡画越发展越丰富,配以各种吉祥物和吉祥词语。"三元及第"与"三元五福"对画,合为"三元五福"。

Pasting drawings of roosters on the door has been popular for a long time. People put this kind of picture on the door to safeguard the whole family. This tradition has continued and people now use a variety of other auspicious animals and phrases.

福禄寿喜财
中华五福吉祥图典

禄

三元及第

Three top students in the imperial examinations

High Salary
Designs of Chinese Blessings

　　明代科举，分别以殿试前三名为"三元"，即状元、榜眼、探花。清代科举，以乡试、会试、殿试的第一名为解元、会元、状元，又称"三元"。"及第"即榜上有名，落榜者为"落第"。三元及第，是家中头等喜事，亦称"三元报喜"。

　　In the Ming Dynasty, the three top students of the palace examination were called the Zhuàng Yuán, Bǎng Yǎn and Tàn Huā. In the Qing Dynasty, the top three students in the three levels of county, provincial and palace were respectively called Xiè Yuán, Huì Yuán and Zhuàng Yuán. This phrase means that having a child being the top student of the palace examination is the happiest thing for a family.

福禄寿喜财
中华五福吉祥图典

三元报喜

The announcement of a top student in the imperial examinations

High Salary
Designs of Chinese Blessings

明朝李东阳诗："本朝科甲重三元。"图中一妇女手捧果盘，内有圆桔三个，表示"三元"。花下喜鹊飞翔"报喜"。接受三个圆桔的妇女身后有一儿童，寓意儿童从小刻苦读书，经得"十年寒窗苦"，长大必能考取第一名。

In this picture, a woman carries a fruit plate which has three oranges in it. This hints at the three top students in the palace examination. The magpie flying among the flowers means the spreading of good news. The child behind this woman means that a child who studies hard will become a top student in ten years.

福禄寿喜财
中华五福吉祥图典

禄

大人虎变

Unpredictable changes of powerful people

High Salary
Designs of Chinese Blessings

《易·革》:"大人虎变,其文炳也。"《疏》:"损益前王,创制立法,有文章之美,焕然可观,有似虎变,其文彪炳。"旧时常以"大人虎变",比喻大人物行止屈伸高深莫测,犹如虎之花纹,斑驳多彩。也喻事业奋发有成。

This term was often used in the old days to refer to the unpredictable behavior of famous and powerful people. This also means great achievement in one's career.

福 禄 寿 喜 财

中华五福吉祥图典

孔子讲学

Confucius teaching

High Salary
Designs of Chinese Blessings

孔子，中国春秋末期伟大的思想家和教育家，儒家学派的创始人。孔子是中国历史上开私人讲学风气的教育家。他约在三十岁时即开始从事教育活动。相传其弟子三千，贤人七十二。他的教育思想十分丰富，被誉为"万世师表"。

Confucius was a great thinker and educator at the end of the Spring and Autumn Period, as well as the founder of Confucianism. Confucius was the first educator to open a private school in Chinese history. He was only thirty when he started teaching. It was said that he had taught more than three thousand students, and that there were 72 outstanding students among them. He was considered the master of all teachers with his rich educating concepts and epigrams.

福禄寿喜财
中华五福吉祥图典

夕牛望日

An old ox looks at the sun

High Salary
Designs of Chinese Blessings

　　曹操《龟虽寿》诗："老骥伏枥，志在千里，烈士暮年，壮心不已。"《三字经》："若梁灏，八十二；对大廷，魁多士。"梁灏八十岁高龄中状元。"夕牛"示老年，"望日"示蟾宫折桂，寓意虽已暮年，但不坠青云之志。

　　It is recorded that Liang Hao came in at the top of the list of successful candidates in the imperial examination when he was eighty. This means that civilian and military officials will not give up their dreams, even in old age.

马上封侯

Immediately become a high official

High Salary
Designs of Chinese Blessings

据《礼记·王制》载："王者制禄爵，公、侯、伯、子、男五等。"侯爵，为五等爵位的第二等，是仅次于公的爵位，在此指高官厚禄。图中猴骑于"马上"，"蜂"谐音"封"，"猴"谐音"侯"，合为"马上封侯"，寓意很快就要被封为高官。

A marquis was the second highest ranking lord among the five rankings lords. Here it represents high office and a good salary. In the picture, the monkey is riding on the horse, which implies immediately winning a good position and salary, because monkey sounds like lord and the phrase on the horse sounds like immediately in Chinese.

福 禄 寿 喜 财
中华五福吉祥图典

云龙风虎

Dragon of the cloud,
tiger of the wind

High Salary
Designs of Chinese Blessings

《说文解字》:"龙,鳞虫之长。"龙,被华夏先民奉为神祖,是中国最尊崇的神物。《说文解字》:"虎,山兽之君也。"《风俗通》:"虎为阳物,百兽之长也。"古有"真龙天子"、"虎将"之说。以"云龙风虎"比喻杰出的人物。

The dragon is worshipped as the ancestor of the Chinese people and the most respectable animal in China. The tiger is considered the king of all animals. The dragon and tiger are often used to refer to outstanding people.

福 禄 寿 喜 财
中华五福吉祥图典

太师少师

Old and young imperial teachers

High Salary
Designs of Chinese Blessings

太师少师为辅导太子的官。西晋设太师、太傅、太保，太子少师、少傅、少保，称为三师、三少。北朝魏、齐沿设，隋以后历代不改。明、清以朝臣兼任，三师三少成虚衔。"狮"谐"师"，图中的大狮小狮喻太师少师，示代代高官。

This is the title of those who gave lessons to the princes. This title was used from the Northern Wei Dynasty until the Sui Dynasty. In the Ming and Qing dynasties these positions were held by government officials. The big and small lions in the picture stand for generations of senior officials.

福禄寿喜财

福 禄 寿 喜 财
中华五福吉祥图典

禄

太师童子

Old and young imperial teachers

High Salary
Designs of Chinese Blessings

在周朝，立太师、太傅、太保为三公，太师最为尊贵，故民间常把狮子喻为太师。少师也是官位，常把小狮子喻为少师。以太师、少师比喻父子为官、代代为官。图以童子戏大狮、小狮，表示长大能金榜题名，身居高官。

In the Zhou Dynasty, Tài Shī, Tài Fù and Tài Bǎo were respectably called Sān Gōng (three officials). Among these three, Tài Shī is the most respectable. Ordinary people used lions to refer to Tài Shī since lion and shī sound alike in Chinese. Tài Shī was also a type of government official. People used big lion and small lion to refer to a father and son both becoming government officials. The children playing with the lions in this picture shows that when the child grows up he will become a senior official as well.

福禄寿喜财
中华五福吉祥图典

五 瑞

Five propitious kinds of jade

High Salary
Designs of Chinese Blessings

《白虎通·文质》:"何谓五瑞?谓圭、璧、琮、璜、璋也。"以五种瑞玉,表示吉庆祥瑞。另《周礼·典瑞》:"公执桓圭,侯执信圭,伯执躬圭,子执毂璧,男执蒲璧。是圭璧为五等之瑞,诸侯执以为王者瑞信,故称瑞也"。

These five kinds of jade were carried by officials of different ranks when reporting good tidings to the emperor, thus they were considered propitious signs for celebration and luck.

福禄寿喜财
中华五福吉祥图典

五子登科

Five sons passing the imperial examinations

High Salary
Designs of Chinese Blessings

《宋史·窦仪传》:"窦禹钧五子,仪、俨、侃、偁、僖,相继登科。"窦禹钧品学出众,为人仗义方正,捐资办义塾,礼聘名师,造就不少人才。且家教甚严,五子均金榜题名。图中以五只小鸡寓五子,以"登棵"谐音"登科"。

It was said that Dou Yujun was an outstanding scholar and also a righteous man who sponsored the construction of schools. He not only employed well-known teachers, and thus produced a lot of talented figures but was also very strict with his own five sons. Later, all five of his sons passed the palace examination and became officials. The five chicks in the picture are metaphors for his five sons.

福禄寿喜财
中华五福吉祥图典

禄

五子连登

Five sons passing the imperial examinations

High Salary
Designs of Chinese Blessings

　　五子登科也称五子连登。《三字经》："窦燕山，有义方，教五子，名俱扬。养不教，父之过。教不严，师之惰。子不学，非所宜。幼不学，老何为？玉不琢，不成器。人不学，不知义。"窦燕山教子有方，五子学而优则仕。

　　This was also from the story of Dou Yujun who successfully educated his five sons. According to ancient Chinese morals, if the children did not behave well, the father should be blamed; if the children were not educated properly, the teacher should be blamed for laziness.

福 禄 寿 喜 财
中华五福吉祥图典

禄

五子连科

Five sons passing the imperial examinations

High Salary
Designs of Chinese Blessings

　　五子登科又称五子连科。窦禹钧是五代后晋时人，所居地幽州属故燕地，故称"窦燕山"。他有五个儿子，长子仪，为礼部尚书；次子俨，为礼部侍郎；三子侃，为补阙；四子偁为谏议大夫；五子僖，为起居郎。均有名于世。

　　Dou Yujun was also called Dou Yanshan, as he lived in the land of Yan. His five sons all became very high officials. His eldest son even became the minister of the Department of Protocol, and all five of his sons were famous people in history.

五子日升

Five sons like the rising sun

High Salary
Designs of Chinese Blessings

《诗经·小雅·天宝》："如月之恒，如日之升，如南山之寿。"像太阳刚刚升起来一样，比喻五子有广阔的发展前途。成语有句："如日方升"、"日升月恒"。五子通过父教、勤学，长大成名出仕，则是"如日中天"，万人景仰。

This means the five sons all have promising futures, just like the rising sun. This term originated from the story of Dou Yujun.

福禄寿喜财
中华五福吉祥图典

禄

五子夺冠

Five sons become champions

High Salary
Designs of Chinese Blessings

冠，是位居第一。《汉书·魏相丙吉传赞》："萧曹为冠。"冠又是冠冕，是仕宦的代称，《北史·寇洛等传论》："冠冕之盛，当时莫与比焉。"图中"五子夺冠"，冠是为官之帽，"冠"又与"官"谐音，意为五子从小有远大理想。

Champion was a term used to refer to officials in Chinese history. In the picture, the hat is a metaphor for those officials since hat and official sound similar in Chinese. This means that these five sons were ambitious when they were young.

福 禄 寿 喜 财
中华五福吉祥图典

禄

五子夺莲

Five sons compete for the lotus

High Salary
Designs of Chinese Blessings

《群芳谱》："凡物先华而后实，独此华实齐生。百节疏通，万窍玲珑，亭亭物华，出于淤泥而不染，花中之君子也。"在吉祥图中以莲之高洁喻为官之清廉。五子不仅学优则仕，且誓为清官。"五子夺莲"又有"五子连夺"之意。

In auspicious paintings, the lotus is used to symbolize officials with honesty and integrity. The five sons of Dou Yujun not only excelled in their studies; they were also officials with honesty and integrity.

福禄寿喜财
中华五福吉祥图典

禄

五子夺魁

Five sons become top students

074

High Salary
Designs of Chinese Blessings

科，指科举。登科，为考试及第之意。中国的科举考试制度，起源于隋朝，废止于清末。夺魁，即争取第一名。科举考试称进士第一名为魁甲，即状元。明代科举制度以五经取士，第一名为经魁，五经之魁为五经魁，亦称五魁。

Chinese imperial exams started in the Sui Dynasty and ended with the collapse of the Qing Dynasty. The top student in the national examination is called the Kuí Jiǎ and also the Zhuàng Yuán. They were also called Jīng Kuí in the Ming Dynasty.

福禄寿喜财
中华五福吉祥图典

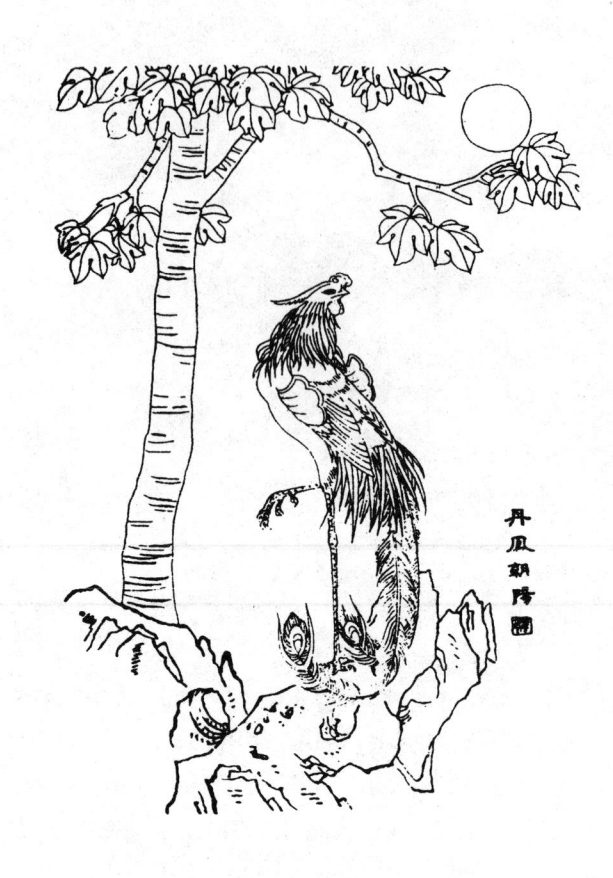

丹凤朝阳

The phoenix flies towards the sun

High Salary
Designs of Chinese Blessings

《诗经·大雅·卷阿》："凤凰鸣矣，于彼高岗。梧桐生矣，于彼朝阳。"凤凰，凤为雄，凰为雌，凤凰为百鸟之长。《史记·日者列传》："凤凰不以燕雀为群。"旧时常以丹凤朝阳喻贤才遇时而起，大展鸿图，前程似锦。

The phoenix is considered to be the head of all birds in Chinese folklore. In ancient times, people used this term to refer to talented and knowledgeable people who showed their abilities when the time was right.

福 禄 寿 喜 财
中华五福吉祥图典

凤鸣朝阳

The phoenix sings towards the sun

High Salary
Designs of Chinese Blessings

凤凰又名丹鸟或丹凤,《辂别传》:"文王受命,丹鸟衔书。""丹凤朝阳"也称"凤鸣朝阳"、"朝阳鸣凤"或"丹山彩凤"等。图主要以凤凰和朝阳组成,有的还配以奇石、彩云、花卉等。"凤鸣朝阳"是稀世之瑞。

These kinds of pictures are characterized by a phoenix and the rising sun. In some pictures there are also precious stones and colorful clouds and flowers.

福 禄 寿 喜 财
中华五福吉祥图典

朝阳鸣凤

The sun rises and the phoenixes sing

High Salary
Designs of Chinese Blessings

凤凰是瑞鸟，是百鸟之王。《大戴礼》："有羽之虫三百六十而凤凰为之长"。《礼斗威仪》："君乘士而王，其政太平，则凤集于林苑。""朝阳鸣凤"是天下太平的象征。凤俱五德，"朝阳鸣凤"也喻贤才遇佳时而起。

The phoenix is considered an auspicious bird and the king of all birds. This term is used to refer to a harmonious and peaceful world. This term also means talented people will become successful when the time is right.

福 禄 寿 喜 财
中华五福吉祥图典

文武状元

文武状元

Number One scholars

High Salary
Designs of Chinese Blessings

　　画中的两位状元，一文一武。文状元纱帽蟒袍，持笏端带；武状元头戴帅盔，手执弓箭。这是一幅清代老北京的门童画，多用在新婚时贴在门上。门童也称门画，类似门神，题材形式比门神多，贴在院内屋室门上之用。

　　There are two Number One scholars in this picture, one in civil service, the other in the military. The former wears a snake embroidered robe; the latter has a sword in hand. This is an old Beijing door painting from the Qing Dynasty and was normally pasted on the gates of a newlywed couple's house.

福禄寿喜财
中华五福吉祥图典

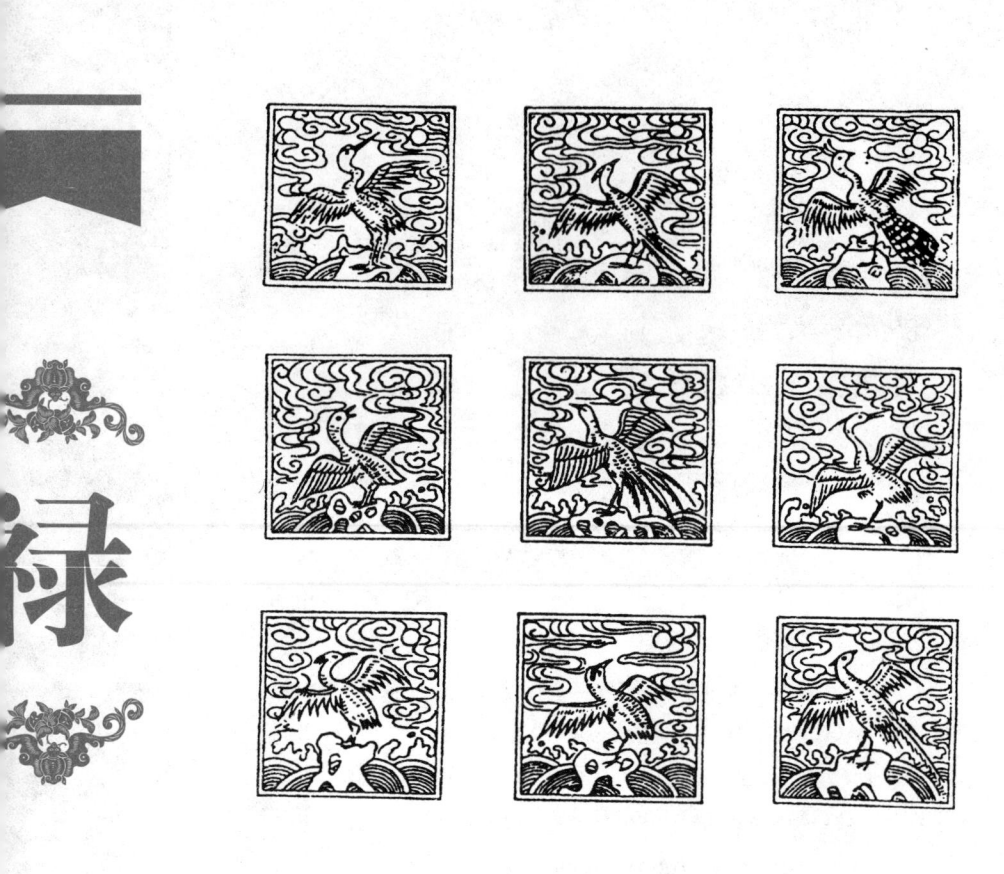

文官补子

The decoration of a civil official's uniform

High Salary
Designs of Chinese Blessings

古代的官服，前胸及后背缀有用金线和彩丝绣成的"补子"，也叫"背胸"，是品级的徽记。清代文官绣鸟：一品鹤，二品锦鸡，三品孔雀，四品雁，五品白鹇，六品鹭鸶，七品，八品鹌鹑，九品练雀。此外，都御史绣獬豸。

People embroidered birds on the fronts and backs of civil officials' uniforms with golden and colored threads. These birds are the symbol of their position. In the Qing Dynasty, nine birds were used on officials' uniforms, which stood for the nine grades of civil rank.

福禄寿喜财

福禄寿喜财 中华五福吉祥图典

禄

武官补子

The decoration of a military official's uniform

High Salary
Designs of Chinese Blessings

《清通典·礼·嘉四》记载，清代武官补子绣兽。一品麒麟，二品狮，三品豹，四品虎，五品熊，六品彪，七品同六品，八品犀牛，九品海马。旧时官服上的补子，是品级的徽记。文官补子上绣瑞鸟图案，武官补子上绣瑞兽图案。

People embroidered animals on the fronts and backs of military officials' uniforms with golden and colored threads. These animals are the symbols of their positions. In the Qing Dynasty, nine animals were used which stood for the nine ranks of military officials.

福禄寿喜财
中华五福吉祥图典

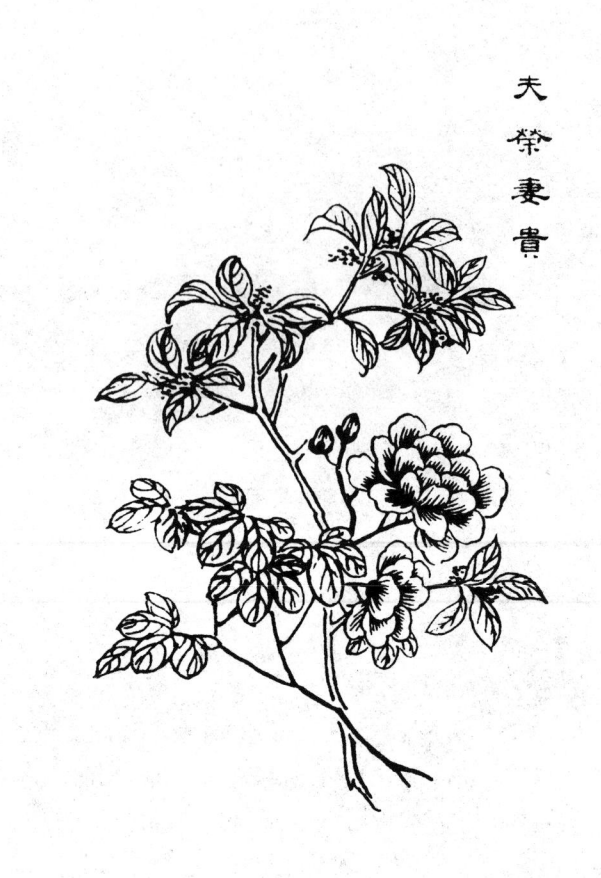

夫榮妻貴

夫荣妻贵

A glorious husband, a noble wife

High Salary
Designs of Chinese Blessings

《诗经·小雅·常棣》:"妻子好合,如鼓瑟琴。"《千字文》:"上和下睦,夫唱妇随。"图以"芙蓉"谐音"夫荣","七"簇"桂"花谐音"妻贵"。合为"夫荣妻贵",寓意夫妻荣辱与共,比翼双飞。婚联:"和睦家庭风光好,恩爱夫妻幸福长"。

The cotton-rose hibiscus in this picture is used to refer to the glory of the husband because of their similar pronunciation. Seven groups of sweet-scented osmanthus represent the noble wife. This term was used to refer to a husband and wife who share weal and woe together.

福禄寿喜财
中华五福吉祥图典

玉树芝兰

The noble magnolia, irises and orchids

High Salary
Designs of Chinese Blessings

　　《晋书·谢玄传》载：谢玄与从兄谢朗俱为叔谢安所器重，安尝诫约子侄："汝等何豫人？"诸子莫言，玄曰："譬如芝兰玉树，欲使其生于庭阶耳。"后世遂将"芝兰玉树"作称颂人才之美誉。在传统文化中，芝兰喻君子，玉树喻人才。

　　This is used to represent talented people. In Chinese tradition, irises and orchids are used to refer to gentlemen, and jade tree means talent.

福禄寿喜财
中华五福吉祥图典

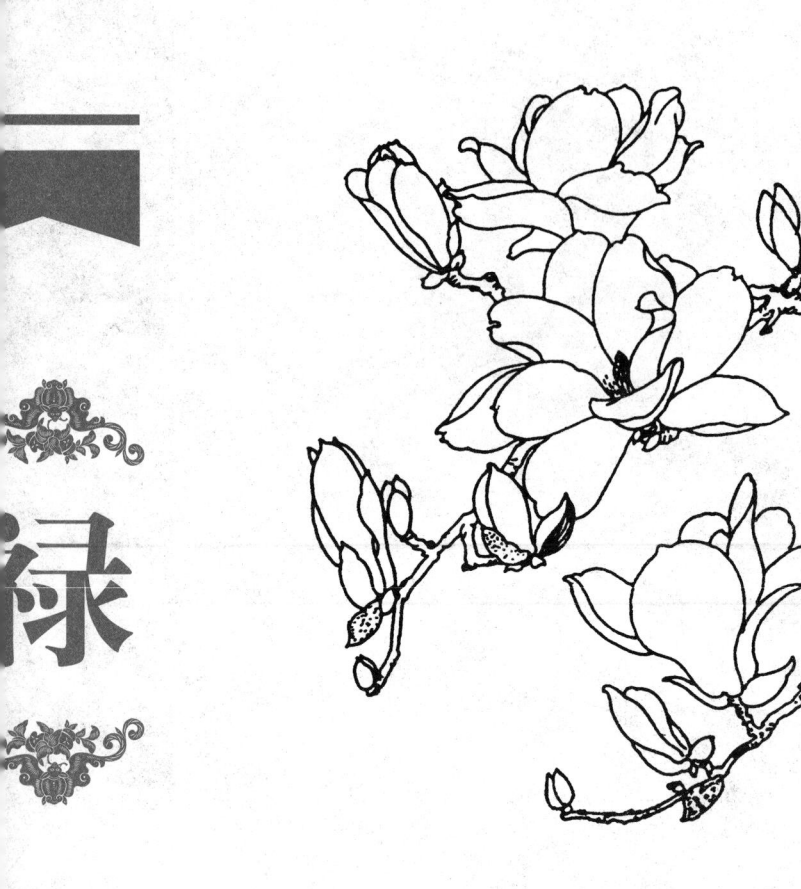

禄

玉树临风

Magnolia faces the wind

High Salary
Designs of Chinese Blessings

　　唐·杜甫《饮中八仙歌》诗句："皎如玉树临风前。"玉兰枝干遒劲，身躯伟岸，吐叶前便绽花，晶莹清丽，犹如玉树于雪山排空而出，气势壮观。这种气势、风格多为古人所称道。以"玉树临风"喻姿貌秀美、才华出众的人才。

　　The magnolia has strong branches and blossoms before new leaves grow. The ancient Chinese people always adored the splendor of this flower. People also use this term to mean good-looking talented people.

福禄寿喜财
中华五福吉祥图典

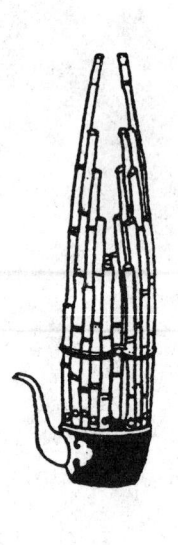

平升三级

Be promoted three grades in succession

High Salary
Designs of Chinese Blessings

平升三级在旧时多作为祝颂加官晋爵之贺词。民间多流传连升三级的故事，平升三级寓意仕途一帆风顺，好运来临三级连升。图中瓷瓶的"瓶"谐音"平"，乐器笙的"笙"谐音"升"，"三枝戟"谐音"三级"，合为"平升三级"。

In old times, this term was used to represent promotion. For the ordinary people, this meant smooth progress in one's career. The *sheng* (a musical instrument) sounds the same as promotion in Chinese, the three-pronged spear as three grades, and bottle has the same pronunciation as level.

福 禄 寿 喜 财
中华五福吉祥图典

平升三级

Be promoted three grades in succession

High Salary
Designs of Chinese Blessings

旧时为官者平步青云，连升三级则是大福。图中的孔雀花翎，是官位、权势的象征。在清朝，官员以孔雀花翎做为冠饰，有单眼、双眼、三眼之分。在清初只赏给少数受皇帝恩宠的王公大臣，后来赏的范围大了，但仍需五品以上。

This was considered to be good luck in the old days. The peacock feather decoration was a symbol of position and power. In the Qing Dynasty, officials liked to use peacock feathers for decoration. In the beginning of the Qing Dynasty, only a few government officials who were favored by the emperor could receive such decoration as presents. Later on, emperors gave this kind of present to more officials, but only officials of the fifth grade or higher.

福 禄 寿 喜 财

福禄寿喜财
中华五福吉祥图典

禄

四艺集雅
Four civilized arts

High Salary
Designs of Chinese Blessings

琴、棋、书、画，是文人的雅兴，也是老年人的乐趣。图中的四位童子祝老人长寿、快乐。"四艺"在中国历史上，有四位代表性的人物。他们分别是春秋时人俞伯牙（琴），三国时人赵颜（棋），晋朝王羲之（书），唐朝王维（画）。

The *qin* (a kind of musical instrument), chess, calligraphy and ink painting were forms of refined entertainment for people of high society and also entertainment for older people. There were four people who were considered to be the representatives of these four arts: Yu Boya of the Spring and Autumn Period for the *qin*, Zhao Yan of the Three Kingdoms Period for chess, Wang Xizhi of the Jin Dynasty for calligraphy and Wang Wei of the Tang Dynasty for painting. In the picture, four children wish longevity and happiness for the old people.

福禄寿喜财
中华五福吉祥图典

加官进禄

加官进禄

Promotion and salary increase

High Salary
Designs of Chinese Blessings

加官进禄不仅是旧时为官者的朝思暮想，也是家长望子成龙的心愿。图中两位妇人盼望两个孩童长大成才，其中一童子手捧官冠，表示"加官"，另一童子手牵一只小鹿，表示"进禄"。旧时春节，民间多将此类画贴于家中，保佑子女。

Promotion and increases in salary were not only the dreams of officials in old times, but also the wishes of parents for their children. In the picture, two women wish that their children could grow up to be officials with a good salary. One child holds an official's hat in his hand, which stands for position; the other child leads a deer, which represents high salary. Ordinary people liked to put such pictures up in their homes during the Chinese New Year for their children.

福禄寿喜财
中华五福吉祥图典

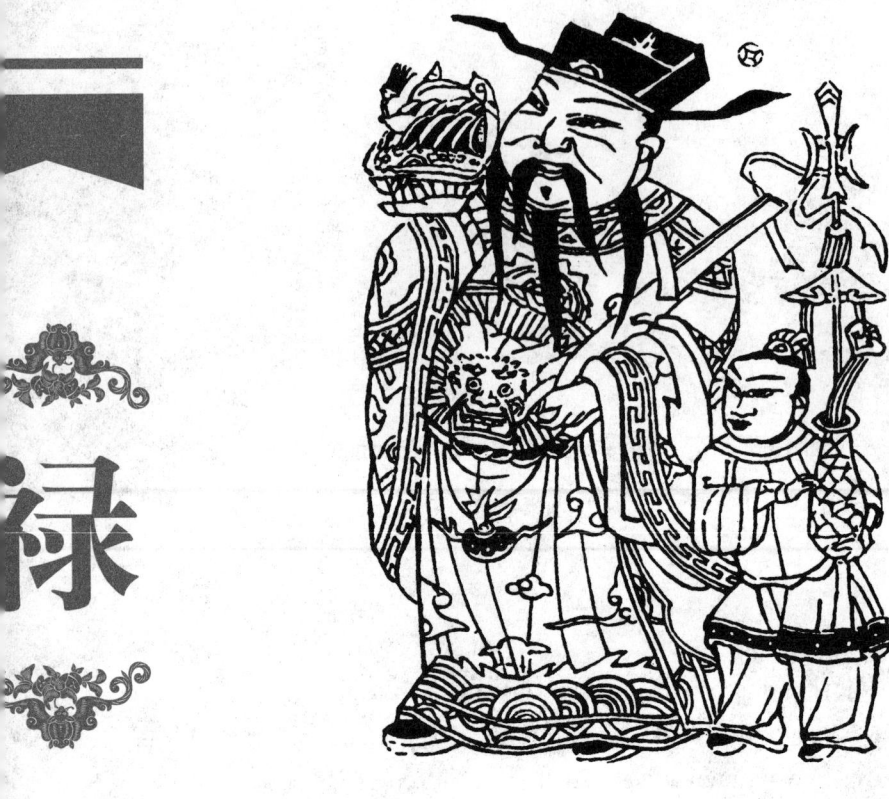

禄

加官进禄

Promotion and salary increase

High Salary
Designs of Chinese Blessings

　　住宅的门多是两扇，故门画是成对的。此图与下面一图是成双的门画，其中一天官手托官冠，示意"加官"，另一天官手托金鹿，示意"进禄"，合为"加官进禄"。两位天官旁边均有一童子持插戟之瓶，表示"平升连级"。

　　There were usually two doors in ancient Chinese houses; therefore the door paintings come in pairs. This picture and the next picture make one pair of door paintings. One official holds a hat, the other a golden deer. These two images combine to mean promotion and salary increase. At each side of these two officials, there is a child holding a bottle with a three-pronged spear in it, which were borrowed for their similar pronunciation to mean continuous promotion.

福禄寿喜财
中华五福吉祥图典

加官进禄

Promotion and salary increase

High Salary
Designs of Chinese Blessings

富则贵，贵则富，富贵二字是不分家的。富，指财丰物富，贵，指官高爵显。禄，即富贵。升官必然增加俸禄，即升官发财。把"加官进禄"的门画贴于家中，因为有百官之长天官的保佑，所以可求得"加官一人之下，进禄万人之上"。

Great wealth is believed to bring about nobility; conversely nobility would bring about wealth. Promotion must come with an increase in salary. By putting promotion and salary increase pictures in their homes, people hope that their wishes will be granted through the blessings of heavenly officials.

福 禄 寿 喜 财
中华五福吉祥图典

禄

加官进爵

Promotion

High Salary
Designs of Chinese Blessings

　　爵是古代的饮酒器，青铜铸，盛于商和西周。《礼·礼器》："宗庙之祭，贵者献爵。"爵也当作礼器。爵的另一个含义是"爵位"，《礼·王制》："王者制禄爵，公、侯、伯、子、男五等。"加官进爵象征官运亨通之福。

　　The jué is a kind of drinking vessel used in ancient China popular in the Shang and Western Zhou periods. Jué were also used as sacrificial vessels. Another meaning of jué is ranks of nobility. There were five levels of rank in old times. This term means that it's a great stroke of luck to be promoted.

福禄寿喜财
中华五福吉祥图典

禄

加官进爵

Promotion

High Salary
Designs of Chinese Blessings

图以一童子手捧三足爵进献给官人，表示"加官进爵"。爵，是古代的酒器、礼器，与爵位的"爵"同形、同音。故旧时吉祥图多以礼器之"爵"表示爵位之爵。官阶的增大，爵位的晋升，是旧时为官者的最大福分。

We see in the drawing that a child is presenting a three-foot *jue* to an official. Jué, meaning drinking vessel and jué, meaning ranks of nobility, are homophones in Chinese. This implies promotion and salary increase. Promotion to higher position and a more senior title were considered to be the greatest fortune to befall officials.

福 禄 寿 喜 财
中华五福吉祥图典

玉女常怀及第郎

玄女送子

A child-sending goddess

High Salary
Designs of Chinese Blessings

玄女，又称九天玄女，中国古代神话中的女神。后为道教所信奉。相传人面鸟身，为圣母元君弟子，黄帝的师父。到了宋朝，九天玄女成了扶助应命英雄、授以天书兵法的女仙。而明、清之际，玄女又成了送子娘娘，玄女庙中有玉女常怀及第郎。

This is a goddess in ancient Chinese mythology who was worshipped by the Taoists. Record has it that the goddess has the face and the body of a bird, and became the master of the Yellow Emperor. During the Song Dynasty, Xuan Nü was considered a goddess who helped those in need. During the Ming and Qing dynasties, she was worshipped as the goddess who brings children to those who wanted to be parents.

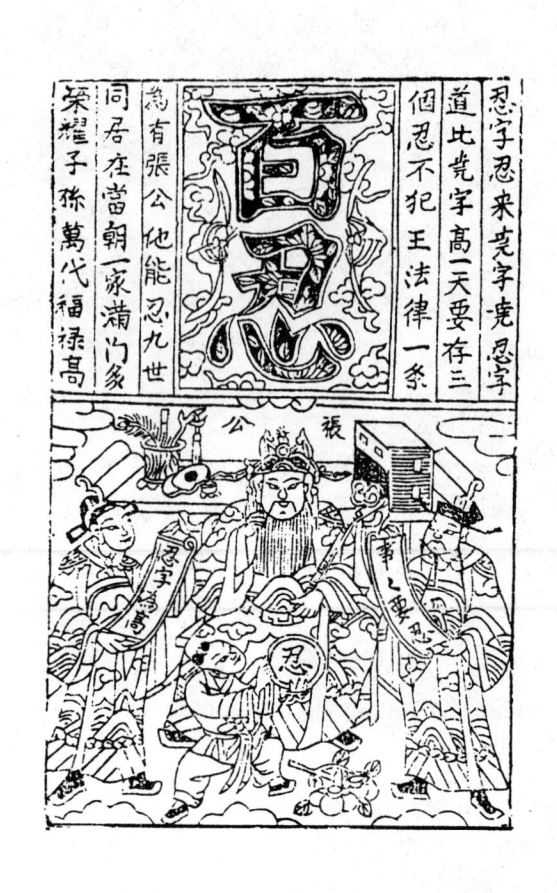

百忍图

The picture of great tolerance

High Salary
Designs of Chinese Blessings

唐高宗幸泰山，经山东寿张，宿于张公艺宅，问及张氏九世同居之本末，张公艺书百"忍"字以对。高宗临行赐以缣帛而去。后人遂以忍字为处世之准。明朝杨枢《淞故述》："百善、百忍二图，邵天骥著。"百忍图元朝已有。

When the Tang Emperor visited Zhang Gongyi on his way to Mount Tai, he was quite amazed at the harmonious cohabitation of the nine generations of the Zhang family. The Tang Emperor asked him how it was possible for such a large family to coexist peacefully; Zhang then wrote the character tolerance one hundred times as an answer. The Tang Emperor thanked him with gifts and left. Later on, people used tolerance to refer to the principle of peaceful living. This type of picture originated in the Yuan Dynasty.

福禄寿喜财
中华五福吉祥图典

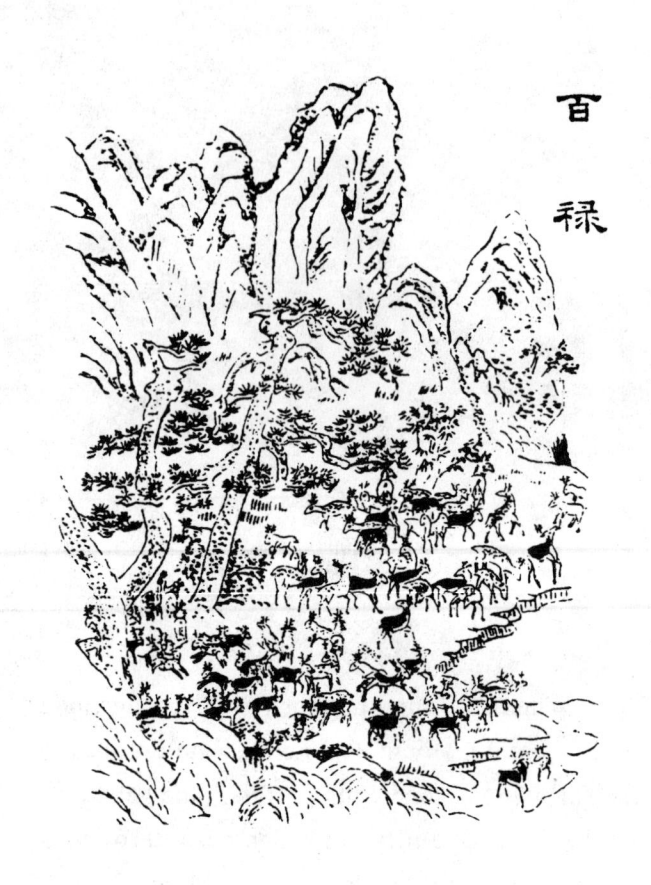

百禄

百 禄 图

A picture of great wealth and good fortune

High Salary
Designs of Chinese Blessings

《抱朴子》:"鹿寿千岁,满五百岁则其色白。"《述异记》:"鹿一千年为苍鹿,又五百年化为白鹿,又五百年化为玄鹿。"又"玄鹿为脯,食之寿二千岁。"鹿为长寿仙兽,可喻"寿","鹿"又谐音"禄",故图以"百鹿"示吉祥富贵。

The deer is an auspicious animal representing longevity in China. Deer is a homophone of high position and good salary in Chinese. This painting means good fortune, wealth and nobility.

福 禄 寿 喜 财
中华五福吉祥图典

百鸟朝凤

One hundred birds pay tribute to the phoenix

High Salary
Designs of Chinese Blessings

凤凰原是一只普通小鸟，在大旱之年，它以辛勤劳动的果实拯救了濒于饿死的众多鸟类。为了感谢它，众鸟从各自身上选一根最美丽的羽毛献给凤凰，从此凤凰就成了一只最美的神鸟，被尊为百鸟之王。每逢它的生日，百鸟朝贺。

The phoenix was said to originally be a small, ordinary bird; but during a drought, the phoenix saved many dying birds with its hard work. To thank him, all the birds took the most beautiful feathers from their bodies to give to the phoenix. Because of this, the phoenix became a beautiful and auspicious bird, and was respected as the king of all birds. Every year on the phoenix's birthday all birds come together to celebrate the occasion.

芝兰竟秀

Irises and orchids compete

High Salary
Designs of Chinese Blessings

　　芝兰合称，常用来喻君子之交。《尔雅翼》："芝，古以为香草，大夫之挚芝兰。与善者居，如入芝兰之室，久而不闻其香，则与之化矣。"兰，自古来就被视为君子或其高洁的品质。芝，是与兰齐名的香草。喻品德好的人竟相媲美。

　　The combination of irises and orchids normally means the acquaintance of a gentleman. The orchid has been used to stand for gentlemen or their noble personalities since ancient times. This term refers to people with high virtue.

福禄寿喜财
中华五福吉祥图典

当朝一品

The Number One government official

High Salary
Designs of Chinese Blessings

图中三位童子，一童子手执如意，表示"事事如意"；另一童子一手执莲、一手执戟，戟也是官阶的象征，表示"连升三级"；还有一童子手执"当朝一品"。童子年小志高，长大不仅要做官，而且要当一品官，一品是最高级别的官。

There are three children in this picture, the first holds an s-shaped jade ornament in his hands, which implies good luck in everything, the second holds a lotus and a three-pronged spear in both hands, which means continuous promotion, the third holds a paper on which is written highest grade official. These children all have great ambitions. They do not just want to become officials, they want to be the Number One official.

福禄寿喜财
中华五福吉祥图典

禄

如意状元
Number One candidate

High Salary
Designs of Chinese Blessings

旧时如考中状元，则有皇家捷报传至家中，名曰："状元及第"。《南部新书》："李翱江淮典部，有进士卢储投卷，翱长女见之，曰：此人必为状头，翱即以女许之，来年果状头及第。"图为清代绵竹门神，贴于房门有状元及第之兆。

In old times, when someone passed the palace examination and became the top student, the royal palace messenger would send the good news to the student's family. This picture characterizes the god of the door in the Qing Dynasty. People liked to paste this kind of picture at the gate of their houses to wish for their children to become the top candidate in the imperial examination.

福禄寿喜财
中华五福吉祥图典

禄

伦叙图

A picture of ethical standards

High Salary
Designs of Chinese Blessings

《孟子·滕文公上》:"使契为司徒,教以人伦:父子有亲,君臣有义,夫妇有别,长幼有序,朋友有信。"此为五伦,即五常,是中国古代人与人之间的关系和应遵守的行为准则。以凤凰、仙鹤、鸳鸯、鹡鸰、莺喻五伦。

The relationships between father and son, monarch and subject, husband and wife, old and young, and that between friends, are generally called the "five ethical standards". These are the Confucian principles of behavior for the ancient Chinese people when dealing with each other. In this picture, five different birds are used as a metaphor for these five ethical standards.

福禄寿喜财
中华五福吉祥图典

旭日东升

The sun rises from the east

High Salary
Designs of Chinese Blessings

　　一轮红日从东海万倾波涛中冉冉升起，象征着国家、事业、生活蒸蒸日上。《剧谈录·慈恩寺牡丹》："初旭才照，露华半晞。"鹤为长寿仙禽，被尊为一品鹤，六只仙鹤有"六顺"之吉，环日而翔，有指日高升之意，又有一品当朝之寓。

　　The red sun rises from the East Sea, which stands for the prosperity of the nation, business and life. The crane is an animal which represents longevity and is also considered to be the supreme bird. Six cranes stand for six kinds of fortune. A crane flying around the sun means progress in the future and is also considered to be a sign of becoming a high ranking official.

福禄寿喜财
中华五福吉祥图典

兰桂齐芳

The orchid and the sweet-scented osmanthus blossom together

High Salary
Designs of Chinese Blessings

　　唐·李白诗："尔能折芳桂，吾亦采兰若。"唐·骆宾王《上齐州张司马启》："常山王之玉润金声，博望侯之兰熏桂馥。"兰花高贵，示为君子。桂花典雅，示为贵人。"兰桂齐芳"寓意集高贵、典雅于一身，或德才兼备之人。

The orchid is considered to be a noble flower, normally used as a metaphor for gentlemen; the sweet-scented osmanthus is elegant and normally represents noble people. This term is used to refer to elegant and noble people, who are capable and have high moral standards.

福禄寿喜财
中华五福吉祥图典

负薪读书

Study from the shoulder pole

High Salary
Designs of Chinese Blessings

汉朝的朱买臣，年轻时虽靠打柴为生，却苦读不辍。他常将书悬于扁担头，边走边读。但不惑之年仍未发迹，妻子崔氏嫌家贫要改嫁，买臣说我五十岁会有大福，妻子不依。天命之年买臣果然为官发迹，衣锦还乡，崔氏羞愧自尽。

Zhu Maichen of the Han Dynasty made his living by collecting firewood, but he never abandoned studying. He often read books while he was walking, hanging books at the end of his shoulder pole (bamboo pole used in ancient China to carry things with). But he did not make any money, and was still poor at the age of forty. His wife wanted to divorce him because she felt ashamed of him; Maichen said that he would make a fortune when he was fifty years old, but his wife didn't want to listen to him. He did make a fortune when he was fifty years old and returned to his hometown in a gorgeous uniform. His ex-wife was so ashamed that she later committed suicide.

福禄寿喜财
中华五福吉祥图典

红杏尚书

Red apricot minister

High Salary
Designs of Chinese Blessings

"红杏枝头春意闹",这著名的咏杏花诗句,是宋朝曾官为工部尚书的宋祁所作,因此后人称他为"红杏尚书"而名扬于世。又每年考进士之际,正值早春二月杏花绽开之时,故又把杏花称为"及第花"。借书与红杏祝科举顺利。

"Spring with red apricots amongst the trees" is a famous sentence from an ancient poem in praise of apricot flowers. It was written by Song Qi, minister of construction in the Song Dynasty. Later, people referred to him as the red apricot minister. People think of the apricot as the flower which brings good luck for students, because the apricot blossoms in February when provincial level exams used to be held. This term is also used to mean blessings of good luck in exams.

福禄寿喜财
中华五福吉祥图典

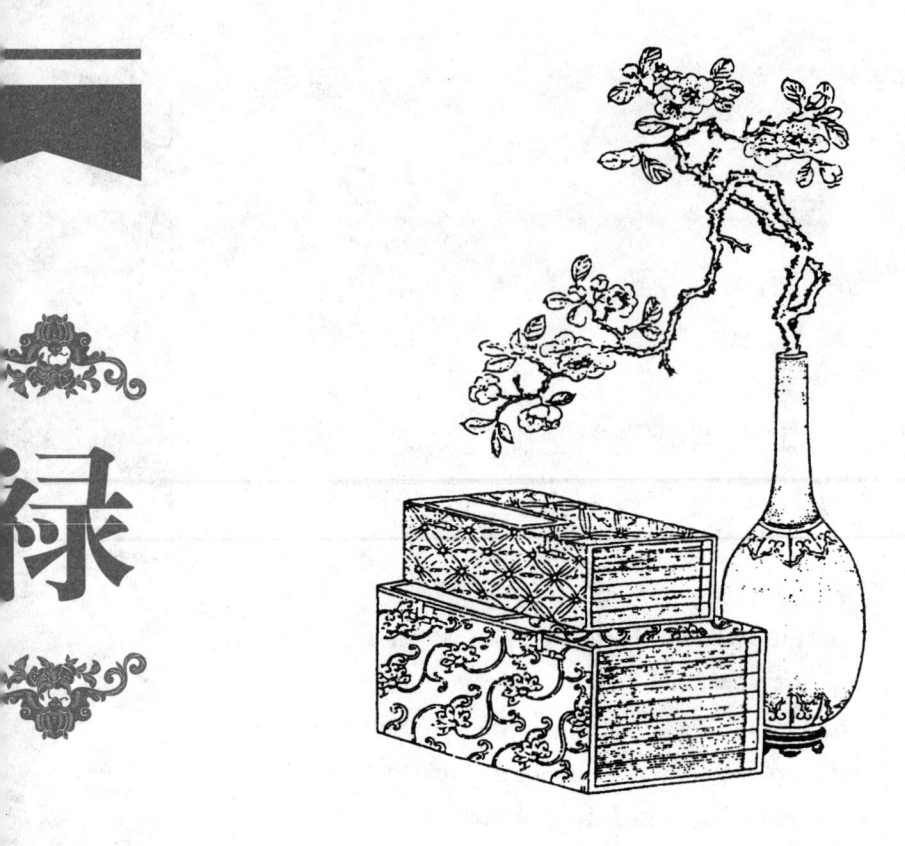

禄

红杏尚书

Red apricot minister

High Salary
Designs of Chinese Blessings

旧时有句："书中有女颜如玉，书中自有黄金屋。""学而优则仕"，书与仕成因果。传说孔夫子讲坛环植以杏，故"杏坛"成了学校的别称，杏花又称"及第花"，杏与学、仕有缘，图中以杏花和书表示"红杏尚书"。

In old times, people linked studying with career advancement and thought they had a cause and effect relationship. It was said that Confucius gave lessons to his students in an apricot arena, which became the nickname of the school. The apricot is also seen as being good luck for students. In this picture, people use books and apricot flowers as a metaphor for this meaning.

鸡群鹤立

A crane among roosters

High Salary
Designs of Chinese Blessings

《晋书·嵇绍传》："或谓王戎曰：'昨于稠人中始见嵇绍，昂昂然如野鹤立于鸡群。'戎曰：'君复未见其父耳。'"晋朝名士嵇绍长得姿容俊美，在人群中如鹤立鸡群。而其父嵇康更是气宇非凡。后以"鸡群鹤立"喻出众。

Ji Shao, a famous nobleman in the Jin Dynasty, was very handsome and referred to as a crane among roosters, though his father was even more handsome than he was. Later, this term was used to indicate outstanding people.

福禄寿喜财
中华五福吉祥图典

苍龙江牙

The green dragon among the tide

High Salary
Designs of Chinese Blessings

《尚书·君奭》疏："凤见龙至，为成功之验。"由此，后世最高统治者被称为"真龙天子"。"海水江牙"是饰于龙袍下摆的吉祥纹样，下面的水谓水脚，上有浪花，水中立石，亦有祥云点缀。"苍龙江牙"喻皇帝一统山河。

The highest ruler was referred to as the True Dragon King in Chinese history. A tidal pattern was the decoration at the lower hem of the dragon robe worn by emperors, on which was depicted water, rocks and lucky clouds. This term is a metaphor for the emperors unifying the whole country.

福禄寿喜财
中华五福吉祥图典

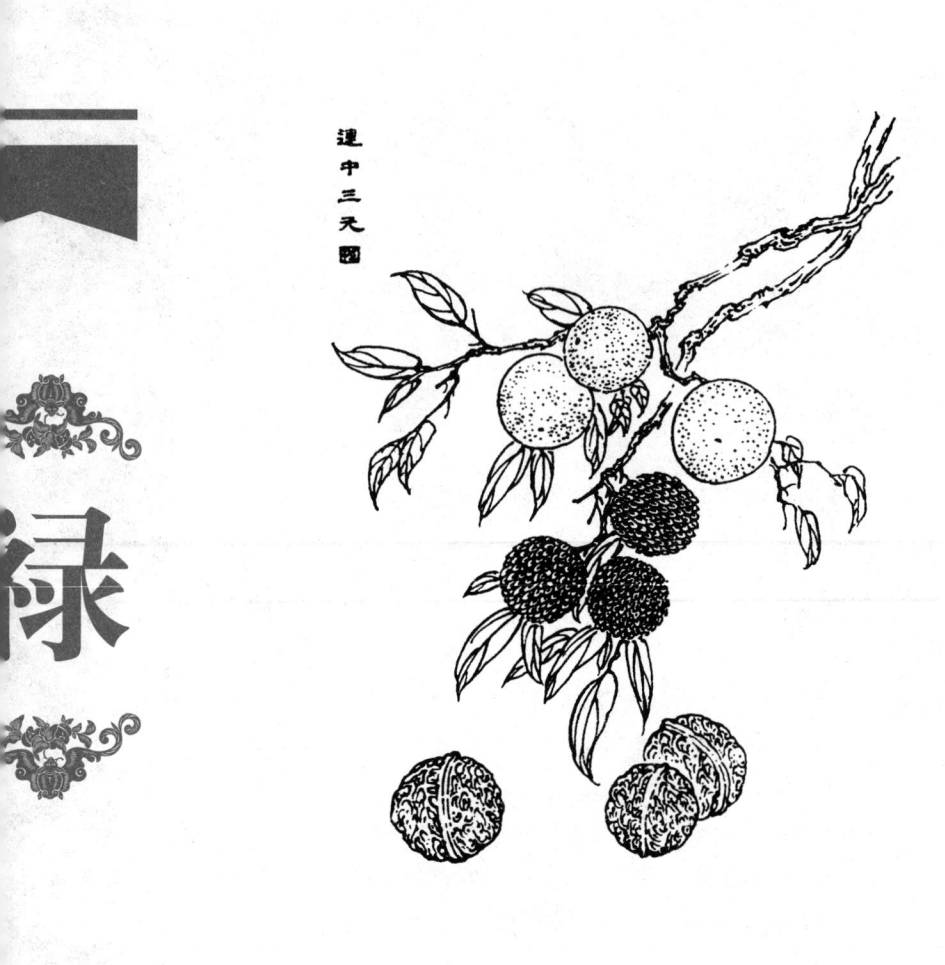

连中三元图

连中三元

Continuous success

High Salary
Designs of Chinese Blessings

旧时科举分乡试、会试、殿试三级。乡试头名称解元，会试头名称会元，殿试头名称状元，合为"三元"。明、清时也以殿试头三名为"三元"。图中以三种圆形果实各三枚喻之。也有以三个元宝或三枚圆形钱币而喻连中三元。

The top students from the county level examination, provincial level examination and the palace examination were called the Three Yuan. In the Ming and Qing dynasties, Three Yuan only referred to the top students of the palace examination. In the picture, three different round fruits symbolize the Three Yuan. As well, sometimes people use three round coins to stand for continuous promotion.

福禄寿喜财

中华五福吉祥图典

连中三元

Continuous success

High Salary
Designs of Chinese Blessings

中国古代钱币多为圆形方孔，而且上面多铸有通宝或元宝等字，如"开元通宝"、"天福元宝"等。图中三童子做射箭游戏，以三枚钱币为的，射中三枚者为"连中三元"。利用吉祥图对孩童进行教育，儿时寒窗苦，长大连中三元。

Chinese ancient coins were usually round with square holes, on which there were Chinese characters. In this picture, three children are playing a game of archery using three coins as targets. Whoever shot all three targets was said to have hit the Yuan three times, meaning continuous success. This kind of auspicious painting was used to encourage children to study hard to be continuously successful after they grew up.

连升三级

Continuous promotion

High Salary
Designs of Chinese Blessings

连升三级，是旧时赞颂仕途顺利的吉语。官升一级都不易，连升三级更是难得之喜。图中瓶中的莲花，与童子击磬之声，谐音"连升"。童子背的玩具三叉戟，谐音"三级"。妇人看着自己可爱的童子，多么盼望他长大连升三级。

This is an auspicious term used to commemorate those who had a smooth career in ancient times, as it is not easy to get even one promotion, let alone three consecutive promotions. The three-pronged spear painted on the child's back sounds like three levels in Chinese. Together with the lotus in the bottle and the chime stone, it stands for continuous promotion. The woman is watching her child playing and wishes that he may have continuous promotions when he grows up.

福禄寿喜财

福禄寿喜财
中华五福吉祥图典

状元及第

The Number One scholar is announced

High Salary
Designs of Chinese Blessings

唐朝举人赴京应礼部试者皆须投状，因称居首者为状头，故有状元之称。中状元者号为"大魁天下"，为科名中最高荣誉。因其为殿试一甲第一名，亦别称殿元。旧时年画中常有"状元及第"，"状元游街"等。

In the Tang Dynasty, all students that took the palace examination went to the capital city to present their examination paper in person. Therefore, the top student was called the head of the paper, being Number One scholar, which is the highest award in any ancient examination. The New Year's pictures of old often show a scene in which the top student is announced.

福 禄 寿 喜 财
中华五福吉祥图典

禄

状元及第

状元及第

The Number One scholar is announced

High Salary
Designs of Chinese Blessings

雄鸡司晨，守夜有时，古帝王以鸡为侯。雄鸡红"冠"，与"官"谐音。图中一童子头戴状元冠，手执"状元及第"，又有"官上加官"之意。其他八位童子，手中都执有与升官有关的吉祥物，如"平升三级"、"加官进爵"等。

The rooster is believed to be able to announce the coming of the morning and guard people at night. As well, cockscomb sounds like official in Chinese. In the picture one child wears a hat in preparation for being the Number One scholar and holds a paper on which is written Number One successful candidate. The other eight children all carry symbols of continuous promotion.

福禄寿喜财
中华五福吉祥图典

状元游街

The Number One scholar parading in the street

High Salary
Designs of Chinese Blessings

　　金榜题名、状元及第，不仅是家中的福分，也是邻里、乡亲的荣耀。旧时，考中状元要骑马游街，乡里同贺。状元在明、清时，是殿试一甲第一名。在唐朝，称进士科及第的第一人为状元。在宋朝，主要是指第一名，有时也用于第二、三名。

　　It was not just good fortune for a family but also for the neighborhood and all the townspeople to have someone pass the palace examination and became the Number One scholar. In ancient times, those who became the Number One scholar would parade through the streets of his town on horseback, while all the townspeople celebrated him.

福禄寿喜财
中华五福吉祥图典

禄

状元祝寿

The Number One scholar celebrating his birthday

High Salary
Designs of Chinese Blessings

科举考试以第一名为元。唐制，举人赴京应礼部试者皆须投状，因称居首者为状头，故有状元之称。中状元者号为"大魁天下"，为科名中最高荣誉。图以"香橼"谐音"状元"，以"竹"谐音"祝"，以绶鸟示寿。意为功名富贵且长寿。

In the picture, people use citron as a metaphor for the Number One scholar. Bamboo sounds similar to celebrate, and the two birds stand for the birthday celebration. This term combines the ideas of glory, fame, wealth and longevity.

福禄寿喜财
中华五福吉祥图典

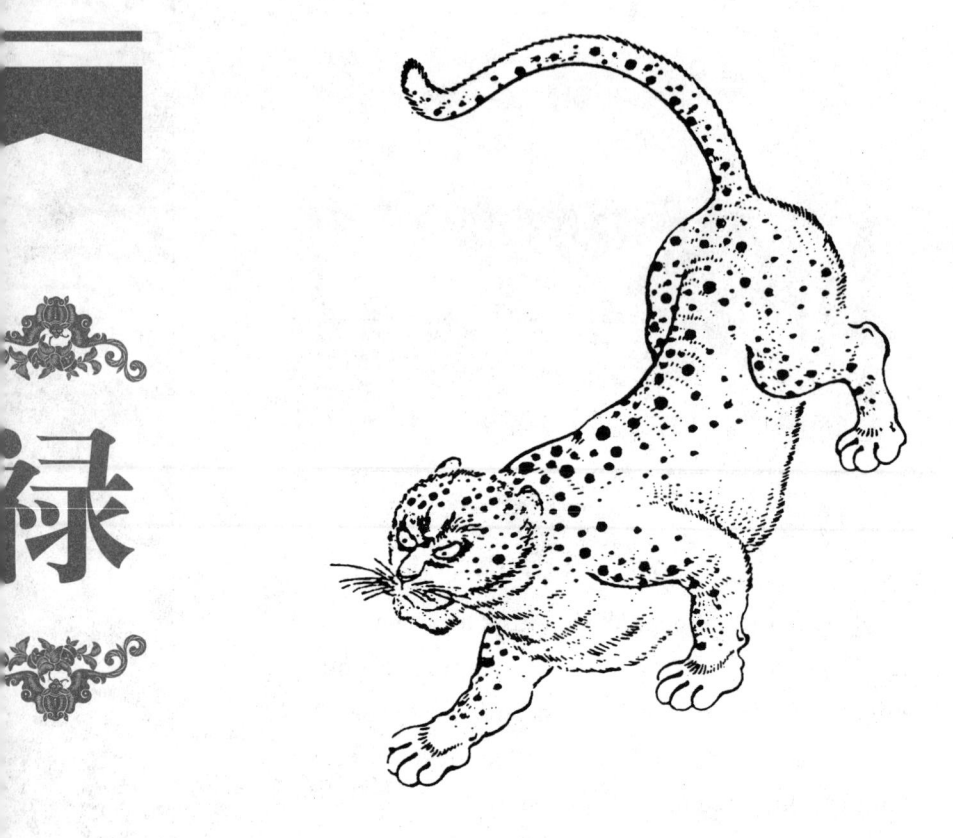

君子豹变

Great changes in position

High Salary
Designs of Chinese Blessings

《易·革》："君子豹变，其文蔚也。"《疏》："亦润色鸿业，如豹之蔚缛，故曰君子豹变也。"喻人的行为有很大变化。《三国志·蜀志·刘禅传》："降心回虑，应机豹变。"指地位上升为显贵。以"君子豹变"颂事业有成。

This term is used to refer to big changes in human behavior, which has something in common with the change of the color and texture of a leopard's skin. Sometimes it refers to the upgrade of one's social position and also can mean great achievements in one's business.

福禄寿喜财
中华五福吉祥图典

禄

平步青云

Stepping over blue clouds

High Salary
Designs of Chinese Blessings

《十州记》:"臣国去此三十万里,国有常占。东风入律,百旬不休,青于干占,连月不散者,当知中国时有好道之君。""青云干占"是吉祥之兆。"平步青云"是旧时祝官运亨通之颂词,与"青云直上"、"青云得路"同意。

This was used to celebrate a blooming career with smooth progress.

福禄寿喜财
中华五福吉祥图典

禄

青龙盘柱

The green dragon surrounding the pillar

High Salary
Designs of Chinese Blessings

龙的形象集中了许多动物的特点，并能兴云布雨，降妖伏魔。是尊贵和权威的象征，是最大的吉祥物，故被中国历代皇帝所专用。在皇宫中处处以龙为饰。一条青龙盘于玉柱之上，且有祥云围绕，象征着帝王的尊严和吉祥高照。

The image of the dragon consolidates many features of other animals. Dragons are also said to be able to chase away evils and demons. In China, the dragon is the symbol of prestige and power, and also considered to be the greatest auspicious animal. Thus, in Chinese history only emperors could regularly use dragon-related items. The green dragon surrounding the pillar symbolizes the dignity of the emperor and is also considered to be a sign of fortune.

福 禄 寿 喜 财
中华五福吉祥图典

青钱万选

Selecting bronze coins from among the pile

High Salary
Designs of Chinese Blessings

青铜钱因年代久远而珍贵，所以在众钱币中万选万中，以此比喻文辞出众。《新唐书·张荐传》："员外郎员半千数为公卿，称鷟（张鷟）文辞犹青铜钱，万选万中。时号鷟'青钱学士'。"晏殊诗："游梁赋客多风味，莫惜青钱万选才。"

The older the bronze coin, the more precious it is; this term is used to describe outstanding articles and writings.

福禄寿喜财
中华五福吉祥图典

青狮荣华

The lion brings high position and great wealth

High Salary
Designs of Chinese Blessings

《尔雅》："狻麑……食虎豹。"狻麑即狮子。《宋书》："外国有狮子，威服百兽。"狮为百兽之王，因其在百兽中至高无上的地位，也象征着人世间的权势和富贵。"狮"谐音师，图中的大、小狮子，喻童子长大官居太师、少师。

Lions are considered to be the king of all animals and have the most supreme position in the animal world. Lions also stand for fame, wealth and power in human society. As well, lion sounds like master in Chinese. This saying implies that after children grow up, they will become senior civil officials.

福禄寿喜财
中华五福吉祥图典

禄

英雄斗志

The ambition of the hero

High Salary
Designs of Chinese Blessings

雄鸡是英雄武勇的象征,《花镜》云鸡具五德：足博距，武也；见敌能斗，勇也。《梦书》："鸡为武吏，有冠距也。梦见雄鸡忧武吏也；众鸣入门，吏所捕也；群斗舍中，惊兵怖也。"古有斗鸡之俗，图以雄鸡喻英雄之志。

The rooster is a symbol of bravery. Among its five merits are the valiance of its sharp claw and its bravery and skill at fighting. In the old days there was a tradition of cockfighting in China. Roosters in this picture stand for the ambition of heroes.

福禄寿喜财 中华五福吉祥图典

英雄独立

The independent spirit of the hero

High Salary
Designs of Chinese Blessings

鹰为高空猛禽，具威姿，有猛志。又"鹰"与"英"谐音，雄鹰单脚独立，喻英雄独步天下，驰骋四海。《诗经·大雅·旱麓》："鸢飞戾天，鱼跃于渊。"李白诗《独漉篇》："神鹰梦泽，不顾鸱鸢；为君一击，鹏抟九天。"

The eagle is a fierce animal in the sky, with great strength and a fighting spirit. In this picture, the male eagle stands on one foot, which symbolizes the independent spirit of the hero.

福禄寿喜财
中华五福吉祥图典

禄

虎威子孙

*Tigers to guard
the children*

High Salary
Designs of Chinese Blessings

《风俗通》:"虎者阳物,百兽之长也,能噬食鬼魅,……亦辟恶。"旧时,民间有画虎于门驱祟的习俗,端午节戴艾虎辟邪在我国已有上千年的历史。虎还宜官子孙,《太平御览》:"悬文虎鼻门上,宜官子孙、带印绶。"

In ancient times, the Chinese had the tradition of painting tigers on the doors to chase away evil spirits. During the Dragon Boat Festival, people would wear tiger masks on their foreheads for the same purpose. This tradition goes back more than a thousand years in China.

福禄寿喜财
中华五福吉祥图典

鱼龙变化

A fish turning into a dragon

High Salary
Designs of Chinese Blessings

《三秦记》："河津一名龙门，水险不通，鱼鳖之属莫能上。海江大鱼薄集龙门下数千，上则为龙，不上者点额暴腮。""鱼龙变化"即"鲤鱼跳龙门"，鲤鱼多能跃过龙门，于是由鱼变成龙。旧时常以"鱼龙变化"颂人高升。

Ancient record recalls that there was a pass called the dragon gate over a river, and the current there was swift. A fish which could jump over the gate would turn into a dragon, but those who failed would die. Generally, only the carp could make it. This term was often used to celebrate a promotion.

福禄寿喜财
中华五福吉祥图典

官上加官

Continuous promotion

High Salary
Designs of Chinese Blessings

　　"官"的称号始见于周朝。《易经·素辞下》:"百官以治"。鸡冠花,夏秋开紫红色花,成公鸡冠状,以"冠"示"官"。蝈蝈,叫声动听,以"蝈"谐音"官"。此图以蝈蝈在鸡冠花上,表示"官上加官",意为官运亨通,步步高升。

　　The word Guan (the title of the officials) originated in the Zhou Dynasty. Cockscomb flower sounds like official; as does long-horned grasshopper. This picture, with a long-horned grasshopper over a cockscomb flower, refers to luck in career development and continuous promotion.

福禄寿喜财
中华五福吉祥图典

官上加官

Continuous promotion

High Salary
Designs of Chinese Blessings

上图是以鸡冠花上加蝈蝈，表示"官上加官"。此图则是以雄鸡之冠加上鸡冠花之冠，表示"官上加官"。《花镜》：鸡"具五德：首顶冠，文也；足博距，武也；见敌能斗，勇也；遇食呼群，仁也；守夜有时，信也。"

A rooster is painted here with a cockscomb flower over its cockscomb. This picture has the same meaning as the previous one. It uses the cockscomb and the cockscomb flower to refer to continuous promotion. According to ancient records, the rooster has five merits: the grace of its cockscomb, the valiance of its sharp claws, its bravery and skill at fighting, its benevolence and habit of signaling others when it finds food, and its faithfulness in keeping watch at night.

福禄寿喜财
中华五福吉祥图典

官上加官

官上加官

Continuous promotion

High Salary
Designs of Chinese Blessings

蝈蝈叫声悦耳、喜人，旧时民间有养蝈蝈的习俗，养鸣虫已是中国特有的文化。图中两个童子在玩蝈蝈，一个童子在捉蝈蝈入笼，另一童子把蝈蝈放在谷穗上，"蝈"与"官"谐音，两只可爱的小蝈蝈，表示"官上加官"的意思。

The chirping of a long-horned grasshopper is very pleasant. Ordinary people used to keep long-horned grasshoppers in their homes in the old days. This is also one of the symbols of Chinese culture. In the picture two children are playing with long-horned grasshoppers; one is putting a long-horned grasshopper into cage, the other is holding an ear of grain with a long-horned grasshopper on it. Long-horned grasshopper sounds like officials in Chinese, so this term means continuous promotion.

福禄寿喜财
中华五福吉祥图典

官居一品

The highest ranking official

High Salary
Designs of Chinese Blessings

古代官吏的等级，始于魏晋。从一品到九品，共分九等。北魏时，每品始分正、从，第四品起正、从又分上、下阶，共分为三十个等级。一品为最高等级，一人之下，万万人之上。图中蝈立菊上，谐音取意"官居一品"，示高官显禄。

The ranking system of ancient officials started in the Wei and Jin dynasties. There were nine levels in total. The first grade was the highest ranking official, who was second only to the emperor. In the picture, there is a long-horned grasshopper perched on a chrysanthemum, which stands for the nobility and wealth of the highest ranking official.

福禄寿喜财
中华五福吉祥图典

禄

春风得意

Riding over the crest to success

High Salary
Designs of Chinese Blessings

唐·孟郊诗《登科后》:"昔日龌龊不足夸,今朝放荡思无涯。春风得意马蹄疾,一日看尽长安花。"表达了诗人孟郊四十六岁时进士及第的喜悦心情。后人常用"春风得意"寓"进士及第",也指人生中功成名就,踌躇满志之意。

A famous poet of the Tang Dynasty, Meng Jiao, showed his satisfaction and happiness in a poem after passing the palace examination. He was already 46 years old when he passed the palace examination. Later, people often used this term to refer to the ambitions and achievements in one's life.

中华五福吉祥图典　福禄寿喜财

春花三杰

Three spring flowers

High Salary
Designs of Chinese Blessings

　　春联"春夏秋冬春为首，梅李桃杏梅占先"梅花为国魂，严冬独绽报春。牡丹为国花，又为百花之王，一品国色天香。海棠为花仙，花白如雪漫春。梅花、牡丹花、海棠花均为名花，又是春花中出类拔萃者，故有"春花三杰"之誉。

The plum flower is considered to be the spirit of the nation, which blossoms in cold weather; the peony is considered to be the national flower and the queen of all flowers; the Chinese flowering crabapple is the goddess among all flowers and its flowers look like snow. These three flowers are all famous, and outstanding among all spring flowers. They are called the three famous spring flowers.

福 禄 寿 喜 财
中华五福吉祥图典

封侯挂印

Winning the title of duke and the official stamp

High Salary
Designs of Chinese Blessings

　　《汉书·朱买臣传》:"拜为太守,买臣衣故衣,怀其印绶,步归郡邸。"印绶是古代官吏的印章,是为官的凭证。图中枫树的"枫"与"封"谐音,"猴"与"侯"谐音,侯为高爵。印挂于树上为挂印。"封侯挂印"寓意官进爵升之喜。

　　Officials' stamps were evidence of rank in ancient China. In the picture, the maple tree sounds the same as conferring, while monkey sounds the same as the duke, which is a senior position. This term is used to refer to the happiness of being promoted.

福 禄 寿 喜 财
中华五福吉祥图典

禄

带子上朝

Bringing the son to the palace

High Salary
Designs of Chinese Blessings

唐朝元帅郭子仪，进爵为汾阳王，官至极品，幼子郭暧尝随朝站班，亦食官禄。此幅清代襄汾灯画，绘着头戴金踏蹬，身穿蟒袍朝服的郭子仪，旁随捧印的郭暧，意为世代封官受爵不断。带子上朝，世代为官，真是禄星高照。

Guo Ziyi was the highest ranking general of the Tang Dynasty. His youngest son, Guo Ai, was also a government official. This picture refers to those who maintain high rankings and positions from generation to generation, which is a sign of good fortune. This lantern picture was originally from Xiangfen in the Qing Dynasty.

福禄寿喜财
中华五福吉祥图典

禄

带子上朝

Bringing the son to the palace

High Salary
Designs of Chinese Blessings

"将门出虎子",在中国历史上父子以及祖孙三代同时在朝为官的颇多。"带子上朝"则表示父为官、子为官,官带流传。"带子上朝"同时也表示父亲教子有方,福荫子孙。而子则少年有为,真是"自古英雄出少年"。

It is said that a general comes from a hero's family. It was quite popular in Chinese history for a father and son to both be generals, or even to have three generations of generals in a family. This term indicates that the family with one official continues to have offsprings who gain official titles. This term also shows that if a father teaches his son effectively, it can bring good fortune to his children.

福 禄 寿 喜 财
中华五福吉祥图典

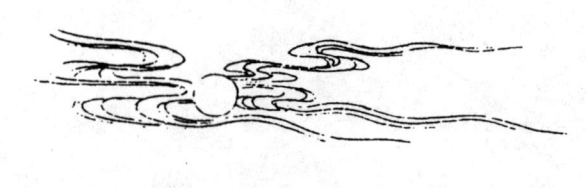

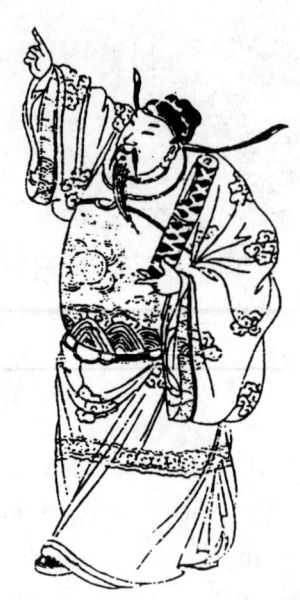

指日高升

Major promotion in a short period

High Salary
Designs of Chinese Blessings

曹植《应诏》诗："弭节长骛，指日遄征。""指日"意为期不远。《周礼》分设六种官职，以冢宰为天官，乃百官之长，统领百官。另外，天官还指道教三官中的"天官"。头戴天官帽，身穿玉带朝服的天官，左手抱笏，右手指日以寓之。

This phrase is used to refer to one who is promoted in a short period of time. In the painting the heavenly official points at the sun, which is a phrase in Chinese meaning the near future. The tablet in his left hand implies power. It combines to imply good fortune in a short period of time.

指日高升

Major promotion in a short period

High Salary
Designs of Chinese Blessings

官高则禄厚，旧时为官者最希望的就是升官发财，盼望早升官、快升官、多升官、升大官。"指日高升"就是很快就要高升了，多用做颂人高升之词。上图以天官指日寓之，此图则以天官手执"指日高升"，颇有天官赐禄之意。

A high position brings a good salary; so a high office and salary was the greatest wish of officials in old times. This picture also implies that the heavenly official will bestow a good salary and a high social position.

福禄寿喜财
中华五福吉祥图典

独占鳌头

The top student in the examination

High Salary
Designs of Chinese Blessings

  鳌，是传说中大海里的大龟或大鳖。唐宋时期，皇宫台阶中间的石板上刻画有龙和鳌的纹饰。凡科举中考的进士要在皇家宫殿台阶下依次迎榜。第一名站在鳌头处，后世称殿试一等一甲状元为"独占鳌头"。后也泛指第一名者。

  According to a Chinese legend, áo is a sea turtle. Patterns of dragons and turtles have been on the doorsteps of royal palaces since the Tang and Song dynasties. Those students who attended palace examinations would wait for results on the doorsteps of the palace, and the top student normally stood at the head of the turtle. Later this term was used to refer to the top student in an examination.

福禄寿喜财 中华五福吉祥图典

独占鳌头

The top student in the examination

High Salary
Designs of Chinese Blessings

鳌头，指皇宫大殿前石阶上刻的鳌的头，考上状元的人可以踏上。后来用"独占鳌头"比喻占首位或取得第一名。图中两童子在做游戏，一童子拉车，另一童子顶冠佩带脚踏鳌头，做"魁星点斗"之状态，以示"独占鳌头"。

This term was used to refer to the top student in an examination. In the picture, two children are playing. One child pulls the cart and the other, wearing a jade pendant, steps on the head of the turtle, which refers to the top student in an examination.

福禄寿喜财
中华五福吉祥图典

香花三元

The three fragrant flowers

浓、清、远、久，是品评花香的四项标准。兰花、桂花、茉莉花，均为上品以馨香著称。在名花中，兰花是观赏花卉中的状元，桂花是食品配料中的状元，茉莉花是熏茶花卉中的状元，故称为"香花三元"。可寓意德、才、貌三全等。

Thickness, clarity, strength and endurance are the four criteria for judging the fragrance of a flower. The orchid, osmanthus and jasmine are all famous fragrant flowers. Among these three, the orchid is considered the top for ornamental purposes; osmanthus is the best for its use as a food additive and jasmine is superior for its aroma therapy usage. These three flowers also mean the gathering of virtues, talent and appearance, respectively.

福禄寿喜财
中华五福吉祥图典

洞天一品

The greatest Dong Tian stone

High Salary
Designs of Chinese Blessings

"洞天一品"吉祥图,画的是"米芾拜石"。旧时官分九品,以一品官最高,位于一人之下,万人之上。吉祥图中有"一品当朝"、"一品高升"等。一品官的补子为鹤,鹤又称为"一品鸟"。能够官至一品是士子的最高追求。

This picture is about the story of an auspicious term, because the first grade is the highest rank, second only to the emperor. The highest ranking official's uniform was decorated with a crane. Therefore, the crane is considered to be the highest ranking bird. An official's greatest pursuit in life was to become the highest ranking official.

福 禄 寿 喜 财
中华五福吉祥图典

禄

前程万里

Great expectations

202

High Salary
Designs of Chinese Blessings

宋·计有功《唐诗纪事·崔铉》："此儿可谓前程万里也。"唐·孟浩然《唐城馆中早发寄扬使君》："访人留后信，策蹇赴前程。"旧时"功名"也称为"前程"。骆驼，性温顺而执拗，善耐饥渴，负重致远。赞颂前程远大。

In old times, fame and achievement were considered to be great expectations. Camels are mild, but stubborn, and can endure hunger and thirst. They can carry heavy burdens for very long distances. This term is used to symbolize great expectations.

福禄寿喜财
中华五福吉祥图典

冠带流传

Retain official titles through the generations

High Salary
Designs of Chinese Blessings

官冠和玉带是古代官位品级的象征，寓意"五福"中的"禄"，即高官厚禄。石榴的"榴"谐音"流"，船形车的"船"谐音"传"，合为"冠带流传"。表示期望上一辈立下的功绩或得到的爵位，能世世代代流传下去。

The hat and pendants of the official are symbols of ancient official levels. This also refers to salary and high positions in the five Chinese blessings. The pomegranate and boat in the picture are used for their similar pronunciation with the phrase passing down. This also means that the achievements and social status of one generation will pass to the next.

福禄寿喜财
中华五福吉祥图典

冠带流传

Retain official titles through the generations

High Salary
Designs of Chinese Blessings

　　当了官是人生的福分，能使官位流传下去，更是祖宗的恩德、家庭的造化。图中两位童子，一位童子一手执鸡，以鸡"冠"示"冠"，一手拉"带"示"带"。另一童子手执石榴谐音"流"。而"船"则谐音"传"，合为"冠带流传"。

　　It was considered to be extremely fortunate to become an official. It was also thought to be respectful to one's ancestors and good for the luck of the family to retain official titles and positions through many generations. In this picture, one of the children holds a rooster in one hand. Cockscomb here implies an official. In his other hand he holds a strip of ribbon, which stands for many generations for their similar pronunciation. Another child holds a pomegranate, which stands for flowing, and boat and passing on to the next generation are homophones in Chinese. All the images combine together to mean continuous fortune.

福禄寿喜财
中华五福吉祥图典

禄

鸾鸟绶带

Golden bird presenting a ribbon

High Salary
Designs of Chinese Blessings

《周礼·天官·幕人》："掌帷幕幄帘绶之事。"《史记》："怀黄金之印，结紫绶于腰。"绶是古代系帷幕或印钮的丝带。印绶常指古代官吏的印章，印是职权的凭证，故以绶带表示功名利禄。鸾鸟口衔绶带象征功名、富贵、吉祥。

Silk ribbons were tied around shields or stamps in Chinese history; stamps were an ancient symbol of officialdom. Therefore, the stamp and silk ribbon stand for fame, glory, wealth and position. The golden bird with a golden ribbon in its mouth stands for fame, glory and luck.

福 禄 寿 喜 财
中华五福吉祥图典

高官厚禄

High position and good salary

High Salary
Designs of Chinese Blessings

《汉书·董仲舒传》:"身宠而载高位,家温而食厚禄。"《孔丛子·公仪》:"令徒以高官厚禄钓饵君子,无信用之意。"以头顶上的高冠(官)和身后的鹿(禄)示高官厚禄。高官厚禄亦称高位厚禄,是旧时读书人的追求。

High position and good salary are the desire of all students in ancient times. The hat and deer in the picture stand for a high position and a good salary because of their similar pronunciation.

福禄寿喜财
中华五福吉祥图典

禄

捧圭朝天

Holding jade facing the sky

High Salary
Designs of Chinese Blessings

捧圭朝天是云南大理白族家中所贴的神像。图中捧圭人为"本主",本主即本境之王,多是白族的英雄或为民有功的先人,本主很受敬奉。圭是古玉器名,长条形。古代贵族朝聘、祭祀、丧葬时所用的礼器,古代的墓葬中常有发现。

This is a religious picture usually seen in houses of the Bai ethnic group in Dali, Yunnan Province. The one who held a piece of jade was the king of Yunnan Province, who was the hero of the Bai ethnic group and the ancestor who most benefited the ordinary people. The jade in his hand is a kind of bar-shaped piece of old jade, which was used as a ritual vessel in sacrificial and funerary occasions in ancient times. It is sometimes found in ancient tombs.

福禄寿喜财
中华五福吉祥图典

翎顶辉煌

The brilliance of peacock plumes and coral

High Salary
Designs of Chinese Blessings

在清朝的冠服制度中，冠上装饰着名贵的红珊瑚和五彩缤纷的孔雀尾，称之为"红顶花翎"。这也是一品官的徽记，一品官位居一人之下，万人之上，官位极品，高贵显赫，故又称之为"翎顶辉煌"，寓官运亨通。

In the Qing Dynasty, officials' formal hats were decorated with precious coral and colorful peacock plumes and were called red hats with peacock plumes. This was also the symbol of the first grade official, second only to the emperor. This saying also implies smooth career development for officials.

福禄寿喜财
中华五福吉祥图典

红顶花翎

A red hat with peacock plumes

High Salary
Designs of Chinese Blessings

孔雀为"文禽",俱"九德"。《逸周书》:"忠、信、敬、刚、柔、和、固、贞、顺。"清朝文官补子中,二、三品皆为孔雀。清代官员以孔雀花翎做为冠饰,"花翎"则是官阶、权势的象征。冠上饰有红珊瑚,更是高官的标志。

Peacocks are said to have nine virtues, which are loyalty, trust, respectability, courage, mildness, harmony, strength, faithfulness and obedience. In the Qing Dynasty, the officials' robe decoration for both second and third ranking officials were peacock patterns and peacock plumes as they were a symbol of position and social status. Higher ranking officials would have coral decorations and peacock plumes on their hats.

福 禄 寿 喜 财
中华五福吉祥图典

海水江牙

Towering peak among the roaring waves

High Salary
Designs of Chinese Blessings

海水江牙，是古代常饰于龙袍下摆的吉祥纹样。图案的下端，向中地排列着许多弯曲的线，名称水脚。水脚之上是翻滚的浪花，并有祥云点缀。高耸的寿石立于浪中，如中流砥柱。意为皇家的一统山河，如柱永固，似水长流。

This is an auspicious pattern used to decorate the lower hem of the emperor's dragon robes. In the pattern there are many rolling waves, together with lucky clouds, while the longevity stone stands in the middle of the water like a pillar. This picture refers to emperors of old who had unified the country and whose sovereignty would be as stable as a pillar of stone and would go on forever, like running water.

福禄寿喜财
中华五福吉祥图典

禄

喜报三元

Magpie announcing the passing of three examinations

High Salary
Designs of Chinese Blessings

"洞房花烛夜，金榜题名时。"是旧时人们生活、事业的追求，是人生喜事。解元、会元、状元，分别是旧科举乡试、会试、殿试的第一名，合称为"三元"。图中的三个桂元，含其"贵"，取其"三元"，与喜鹊合为"喜报三元"之喜。

The candlelit wedding night and the announcement of being on the shortlist of the palace examination were two dreams of ancient people for their lives and careers, and they were considered to be extremely happy events in life. In the picture, three longans together with a magpie represent the happiness of passing three big examinations.

福 禄 寿 喜 财
中华五福吉祥图典

喜得连科

Happily pass the palace examination

High Salary
Designs of Chinese Blessings

宋·苏辙《梁焘转朝奉大夫》："因材任人，国之大柄；考绩进秩，吏之常法。""学而优则仕"，科举考试是通向官场的阶梯。图中以喜鹊示"喜"，以芦苇连棵而喻"连科"。在科举考试中，连考连中，预示仕途光明，前程似锦。

Passing the imperial examinations was a requirement for becoming a government official in the old times. In the picture, the magpie stands for happiness, while the reed sounds like continuous in Chinese. When someone passed the palace examination, it showed that he had great promise for the future.

福 禄 寿 喜 财
中华五福吉祥图典

禄

辈辈封侯

Official position held through generations

High Salary
Designs of Chinese Blessings

　　"背"与"辈"谐音,"猴"与"侯"谐音,寓辈辈封侯为官。另有提倡伦理人情之意。《孝子传》:"余尝至绥安县,逢徒逐猴,猴母负子而没水。水虽深而清,以戟刺之,自胁以下中断,脊尚连。抄着舡中,子随其母傍,以手折子而死。"

　　In Chinese back sounds like generation, and monkey sounds like duke. This term means that a significant official position is kept for many generations. This saying also suggests observing the ethical norms of society.

福 禄 寿 喜 财
中华五福吉祥图典

魁星点斗

Kwei Star pointing to the Big Dipper

High Salary
Designs of Chinese Blessings

　　魁星，是北斗七星中成斗形的四颗星中离斗柄最远的一颗。魁星，也是我国神话中所说的主宰文章兴衰的神。文运与禄运是密不可分的，旧时很多地方都有魁星楼、魁星阁等。魁星，也是道家之神仙，故图的正上方有"八卦图"。

　　The Kwei star is at the tip of the bowl of the Big Dipper. Since one's literary talent is associated with one's position and salary, there were many towers and temples to the Kwei star in different places for people to worship. The Kwei star is also regarded as a god in Taoism, thus an Eight-sided Trigram appears at the top of the picture.

福禄寿喜财
中华五福吉祥图典

禄

禄星高照

The star symbolizing salary shines above

High Salary
Designs of Chinese Blessings

《周礼》设六种官职，以冢宰为天官，是百官之长。道教中有"三官"，其中天官是司官之神。民间传说天上有福、禄、寿三星。高贵的官职、优厚的俸禄，是读书人的终身追求。有禄星高照，自然是"状元及第"、"独占鳌头"了。

It was said that there were three stars in the heaven symbolizing happiness, position and salary, and longevity, respectively. High position and good salary was the life-time pursuit of all students in old times. With blessings at the start, it was believed that those who took part in the palace exam would definitely be number one.

猿猴托印

The monkey brings official position

High Salary
Designs of Chinese Blessings

图为清代河北武强的窗画，左右对称成双，贴于室内窗户两旁。在雕花的石锁上猿猴做出托印、捉蜂、摘桃、攀树等各种寓意吉祥的活动，旁有牡丹花开。"蜂"与"猴"谐音"封侯"，"玉印"示"官运"，合为禄意。牡丹示富贵，桃子示多寿。

This is one of a pair of pictures on both sides of inner windows in Wuqiang, Hebei Province, during the Qing Dynasty. In the painting the monkey is sitting over the carved rock making different auspicious gestures, such as holding official stamps, catching bees, picking peaches and climbing trees, etc. Bees and monkeys together sound the same as granting titles of nobility in Chinese. The blossoming peony beside the monkey means glory and wealth, while peach represents longevity, and the jade stamp stands for good luck in becoming a government official.

福 禄 寿 喜 财
中华五福吉祥图典

富寿年丰

富寿年丰

Enjoy wealth, longevity and good harvests

High Salary
Designs of Chinese Blessings

"富寿年丰"与"猿猴托印"是一对窗画。《礼记》："王者之禄爵，公、侯、伯、子、男，凡五等。"侯是中国古代的爵位之一，猴为灵物，且"猴"与"侯"谐音，故吉祥图中猴多与封侯有关。"猿猴托印"意同"封侯挂印"。

This is the other half of the previous pair of pictures. A duke is one of the ranks of nobility in Chinese history. The monkey is considered to be a type of spiritual animal and also sounds like duke in Chinese. Therefore, monkeys in auspicious paintings usually refer to the rank of duke.

福 禄 寿 喜 财
中华五福吉祥图典

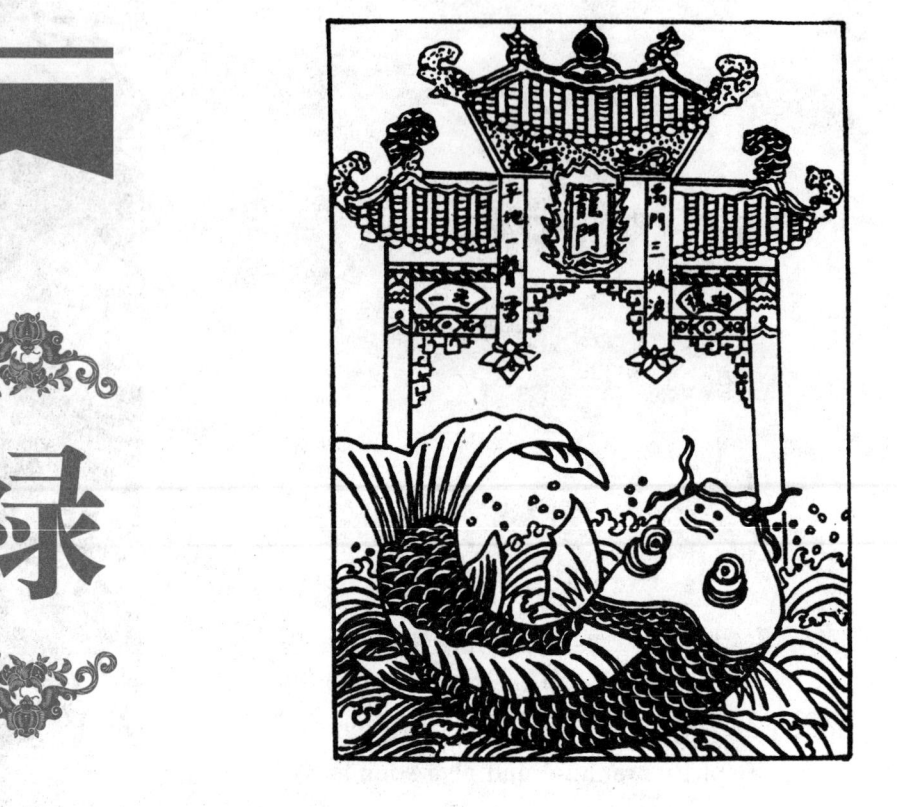

禄

鲤跃龙门

The carp jumping over the dragon gate

High Salary
Designs of Chinese Blessings

《三秦记》:"河津一名龙门,大鱼集龙门下数千,不得上。上者为龙,不上者鱼……"图中龙门上有联:"平地一声雷,禹门三级浪。"横额有句:"一元复始"。一条鲤鱼跃跃欲试,跳过龙门则"平步青云",不过则"曝腮龙门"。

It was said that a carp who could jump over the dragon gate would turn into a dragon. This saying is a wish for a smooth career.

福 禄 寿 喜 财
中华五福吉祥图典

禄

禄位高升

Promotion to an official position

High Salary
Designs of Chinese Blessings

图为清代襄汾的灯画,一位穿戴似太子装束的童子,右手高高托起一盘,有高升之意,另外盘中有一尊爵,"爵"喻"爵位"。童子身旁的一头梅花鹿,"鹿"喻"高官厚禄",合为"禄位高升"。寄予了"学而优则仕"。

This was a lantern painting in Xiangfen in the Qing Dynasty. In the painting, one child in princely dress holds a plate high in his right hand, which stands for promotion, and there is a bronze cup on the plate implying ranks of nobility. Beside the child is a deer, which implies high position and good salary. All the images combined refer to promotion to official positions, which proves that those who excel in their studies will become government officials.

福禄寿喜财

中华五福吉祥图典

攀桂乘龙

Passing the palace examination and getting happily married

High Salary
Designs of Chinese Blessings

攀桂即折桂，旧时称中举为折桂，始于《晋书·郤诜传》。乘龙即乘龙快婿，源于《楚国先贤传》："孙俊、李膺俱娶太尉桓焉女，时人谓桓叔元两女俱乘龙。言得婿如龙也。"攀桂喜乘龙即祝颂新婚之喜，又贺科举折桂。

This term originated in a story from the Jin Dynasty. It was used to represent the happiness of getting married and passing the palace examination simultaneously.

福禄寿喜财
中华五福吉祥图典

蟾宫折桂

Pluck osmanthus blossoms from the moon

High Salary
Designs of Chinese Blessings

　　《淮南子》："日中有跑踆乌，月中有蟾蜍。"《后汉书·天文志》注："姮娥遂托身于月，是为蟾蜍。"故称月为蟾宫。八月桂花遍地开，故八月又有"桂月"之称。《淮南子》："月中有桂树。"旧时称科举高中为"蟾宫折桂"。

　　The Jade Palace refers to the moon in Chinese folklore. August in China is called the season of the sweet-scented osmanthus, because sweet-scented osmanthus blossoms in August. In old times, this term meant passing the palace examination.

福禄寿喜财
中华五福吉祥图典

麒麟送子

Kylin bringing sons

High Salary
Designs of Chinese Blessings

《陈书·徐陵传》:"时宝志上人者,世称其有道,陵年数岁,家人携之以俟之,宝志手摩其顶,曰'天上石麒麟也'。"旧时,赞别人家孩童美称为"麒麟儿"、"麒子"、"麒儿"。"抱来天上麒麟子,送与人间积善家"。

In ancient times in China, people liked to praise the children of other families as sons of kylins. It's said that kylins would bring sons to families of merit.

福禄寿喜财
中华五福吉祥图典

禄

麒麟送子

Kylin bringing sons

High Salary
Designs of Chinese Blessings

在吉祥图中，有的麟子手执"莲"与"笙"，有"连生贵子"之意；有的麟儿手执"如意"和"玉书"，有"麟吐玉书"之意。旧时，小儿佩带的长命锁，有以金银打制成麒麟状的，以寄"麒子麟儿"之意。多生麒麟儿是家中大福。

In auspicious Chinese paintings, children holding a lotus and a *sheng,* a musical instrument, stand for giving birth to sons. Some hold an s-shaped jade ornaments or jade books, which mean the kylin writes books. In old times, children wore long-life locks, a type of necklace, which was made of gold and silver and in the shape of a kylin. This was to hint that the children were the offsprings of kylins. It was considered to be a great joy for a family to have more children.

英文翻译：周　晔
责任编辑：陆　瑜
英文编辑：吴爱俊
封面设计：古　手

图书在版编目（CIP）数据

中华五福吉祥图典. 禄：汉英对照 / 黄全信, 黄迎主编；周晔译. -- 北京：华语教学出版社, 2015.1
　ISBN 978-7-5138-0924-5

　Ⅰ.①中… Ⅱ.①黄… ②黄… ③周… Ⅲ.①图案 – 中国 – 图集 Ⅳ.①J522

中国版本图书馆CIP数据核字(2015)第005965号

中华五福吉祥图典·禄
黄全信　黄　迎　主编
＊
©华语教学出版社有限责任公司
华语教学出版社有限责任公司出版
（中国北京百万庄大街24号 邮政编码100037）
电话: (86)10-68320585, 68997826
传真: (86)10-68997826, 68326333
网址：www.sinolingua.com.cn
电子信箱：hyjx@sinolingua.com.cn
新浪微博地址：http://weibo.com/sinolinguavip
北京天宇星印刷厂印刷
2003年（大32开）第1版
2015年（16开）修订版
2015年修订版第1次印刷
（汉英）
ISBN 978-7-5138-0924-5
定价: 59.00元